"Healing emotional pain is one of the deepest journeys one can make in life—to make peace with yourself and the world. This wise and compassionate workbook points to a way."

—**Bob Stahl, PhD**, coauthor of *A Mindfulness-Based Stress Reduction Workbook*, *Living with Your Heart Wide Open*, *Calming the Rush of Panic*, *MBSR Every Day*, and more

"This book is an excellent resource for working on yourself. I'm especially impressed with how the authors have combined savvy cognitive behavioral modification strategies with superb mindfulness acceptance—integration—resolution skills for difficult emotional states. Very thorough and will be helpful for both novices and those more experienced on the psychological journey."

—**John Ruskan**, author of *Emotional Clearing* and *Deep Clearing*

"*Healing Emotional Pain Workbook* is an artful collaboration of four authors who have developed a highly effective, integrative approach to self-healing. Get this practical, research-based workbook. Do the revealing self-assessment and complete the comprehensive worksheets to heal the emotional pain that has been keeping you stuck."

—**Paul Aurand, MHt**, author of *Essential Healing*, and award-winning master hypnotherapist who has worked in the field for more than thirty years

"This book is an excellent, practical companion and support for anyone who wishes to take better control of their own life—especially their inner life and the often-disturbing personal experiences of emotional pain. The authors have provided a tremendous resource that is easy to access and utilize, while also revealing an achievable pathway toward necessary healing. Based in science and established research, this book is also an invitation to move beyond healing as the only goal, and to discover the beautiful possibility of a happier, more compassionate, and wiser life."

—**Jeffrey Brantley, MD**, emeritus consulting professor in Duke University Medical Center's department of psychiatry and human behavior, and author of *Calming Your Anxious Mind*

"*Healing Emotional Pain Workbook* offers an integration of skills and perspectives cultivated from the best of mindfulness-infused Western psychology. The exercises provide access to the underlying sense of wellness and agency we all carry within us, when not identified with our negative thought patterns. Highly recommended for those desiring to know the truth of who they are, free from the conditioning of maladaptive beliefs."

> —**Kate Gustin, PhD**, clinical psychologist, founder of PoZitive Strides psychoeducational services, and author of *The No-Self Help Book*

"Survivors of abuse desperately need help when it comes to finding safer and more effective coping mechanisms. This well-written and organized workbook offers powerful strategies such as distress tolerance skills, emotion acceptance, and flexible thinking skills along with teaching important practices such as mindfulness, self-compassion, patience, serenity, and relapse prevention. I highly recommend it if you are a survivor of childhood abuse or adult emotional, physical, or sexual abuse."

> —**Beverly Engel, LMFT**, author of *Healing Your Emotional Self*

"*Healing Emotional Pain Workbook* will be a go-to book for anyone looking to find their wise mind when emotional intensity, anxiety, or depression derail you from your own goals and values. With dozens of tools and self-reflection worksheets, you can learn to navigate what the authors call 'emotional storms.' The case examples make understanding and applying these tools easy to do. This is a terrific tool kit!"

> —**Lara Honos-Webb, PhD**, author of *Six Super Skills for Executive Functioning* and *The Gift of Adult ADD*

Healing Emotional Pain Workbook

PROCESS-BASED CBT TOOLS FOR MOVING BEYOND SADNESS, FEAR, WORRY & SHAME TO DISCOVER PEACE & RESILIENCE

MATTHEW MCKAY, PHD · PATRICK FANNING
ERICA POOL, PSYD · PATRICIA E. ZURITA ONA, PSYD

New Harbinger Publications, Inc.

Publisher's Note

This publication is designed to provide accurate and authoritative information in regard to the subject matter covered. It is sold with the understanding that the publisher is not engaged in rendering psychological, financial, legal, or other professional services. If expert assistance or counseling is needed, the services of a competent professional should be sought.

Distributed in Canada by Raincoast Books

Copyright © 2022 by Matthew McKay, Patrick Fanning, Erica Pool, and Patricia E. Zurita Ona
New Harbinger Publications, Inc.
5674 Shattuck Avenue
Oakland, CA 94609
www.newharbinger.com

Cover design by Sara Christian

Cover photo by Willian Justen de Vasconcellos on Unsplash.

Acquired by Catharine Meyers

Edited by Rona Bernstein

Library of Congress Cataloging-in-Publication Data

Names: McKay, Matthew, author. | Fanning, Patrick, author. | Pool, Erica, author. | Zurita Ona, Patricia, author.

Title: Healing emotional pain workbook : process-based CBT tools for moving beyond sadness, fear, worry, and shame to discover peace and resilience / Matthew McKay, Patrick Fanning, Erica Pool, and Patricia E. Zurita Ona.

Description: Oakland, CA : New Harbinger Publications, Inc., [2022] | Includes bibliographical references.

Identifiers: LCCN 2021048270 | ISBN 9781648480218 (trade paperback)

Subjects: LCSH: Psychic trauma. | Psychic trauma--Treatment. | Cognitive therapy.

Classification: LCC RC552.T7 M355 2022 | DDC 616.85/2106--dc23/eng/20211116

LC record available at https://lccn.loc.gov/2021048270

Printed in the United States of America

24   23   22

10   9   8   7   6   5   4   3   2   1   First Printing

Contents

Introduction

This workbook will teach you how to heal the emotional pain in your life—the depression, anxiety, shame, fear, anger, and other painful feelings that keep you stuck and unhappy. Guided by an approach called process-based cognitive behavioral therapy, you will learn how to

1. identify and understand your unique emotional coping style—the *mechanisms* that create enduring emotional pain; and

2. harness *change processes* that will enable you to

    - reduce the intensity and frequency of painful feelings,

    - overcome the effects of negative thoughts,

    - make choices based on your values rather than emotions, and

    - stop avoiding life and start living.

Negative Coping Mechanisms

Everyone learns ways to cope with stress and emotional pain. Some of them help; some of them have the long-term effect of worsening your emotional pain. These are called *transdiagnostic coping mechanisms*. They create the enduring emotional pain that you experience as persistent anger, shame, or emotion dysregulation or that gets diagnosed as specific disorders such as anxiety, depression, or posttraumatic stress disorder (PTSD).

Researchers have studied transdiagnostic coping mechanisms as a cause of chronic emotional pain for almost two decades (Barlow, Allen, and Choate 2004; Frank and Davidson 2014; Harvey, Watkins, and Mansell 2004; McKay, Zurita Ona, and Fanning 2012; Nolen-Hoeksema and Watkins 2011) and have identified eleven mechanisms most responsible for emotional disorders. These negative coping mechanisms are:

- behavioral avoidance

- safety seeking

- emotion-driven behavior

- distress intolerance

- emotion avoidance

- thought avoidance

- cognitive misappraisals

- self-blame (internalizing)

- blaming others (externalizing)

- worry

- rumination

Following this introduction, you'll complete an assessment to identify which negative coping mechanisms you frequently use and begin to learn how they affect you emotionally. Almost no one uses all eleven coping mechanisms; most people tend to use particular mechanisms while making little use of others. When you understand which mechanisms you use to cope with stress and emotional pain, you'll get a glimpse of what needs to change and how you can begin healing your emotional distress.

So step one is knowing the things you do that make your emotions more intense and long-lasting. And step two is learning the change processes that will liberate you from the struggle with strong feelings and instead create full engagement with life.

Change Processes

Cognitive behavioral therapy (CBT) has been developing *change processes*—ways to promote change—for fifty years (Mahoney 1974). The change processes in this book that are focused on reducing negative coping mechanisms have been extensively tested and empirically validated (Frank and Davidson 2014; Hayes and Hofmann 2018). The evidence is strong. These change processes work and will help heal your emotional pain. For example, let's look at two of the ten change processes in this workbook: behavioral activation and situational exposure.

Behavioral Activation

Depression leads individuals to shut down and withdraw from relationships, tasks, challenges, and even pleasurable activities. The result, research shows, is that life is less and less rewarding and the individual spirals down into deeper levels of sadness and disengagement. The change process known as *behavioral activation* reverses this process, helping people schedule weekly activities that are pleasurable, values-based, and helpful in mastering the tasks of life. The result is an upward spiral as the formerly depressed person becomes more and more engaged in life. Research shows that the process of behavioral activation reduces depression dramatically in most people.

Situational Exposure

Anxiety drives individuals to withdraw from situations and challenges that frighten them. But research shows that the result is more anxiety, leading to a diminished sense of safety and efficacy in the face of challenging situations. The change process of *situational exposure* reverses the fear experience, teaching people that facing anxiety-evoking situations is ultimately less painful than trying to avoid them. Hundreds of studies show that situational exposure reduces anxiety and frees you to live a greatly expanded life.

What Is Process-Based Cognitive Behavioral Therapy?

Traditional CBT begins with a diagnosis of a "disorder," such as social anxiety or depression, and then provides an evidence-based therapy protocol to treat it. The problem with treating disorders, as CBT has done, is the failure to address and target the root cause of emotional problems—negative coping mechanisms. Merely treating symptoms such as anxiety or depression is like taking an aspirin to reduce pain for a problem caused by an infection. You have to treat the *source* of the problem for things to permanently improve. This book will help you identify and treat the root cause of your chronic emotional pain.

Consider this fact: depression co-occurs with anxiety 60 percent of the time. If you're anxious, you are also likely to be depressed. Why would such different emotional problems show up together? The answer is that many of the same negative coping mechanisms that cause anxiety (worry, rumination, behavioral avoidance, safety seeking, emotion-driven behavior, and emotion avoidance) also drive depression. To treat co-occurring depression and anxiety, you have to treat the mechanisms that cause both. This book will teach you how to do exactly that.

Rather than treating a disorder, process-based CBT is about targeting and reducing negative coping mechanisms with positive change processes (Hayes and Hofmann 2018) while building strengths to fully engage with life (Cloninger 1999; Seligman and Csikszentmihalyi 2000). Strength-based change processes have deep roots in Buddhist and other contemplative traditions, with strong empirical evidence for their effectiveness (McKay and Wood 2019). It often isn't enough just to reduce old negative mechanisms; it's also important to build strengths to help you turn toward life, toward a commitment to what Jon Kabat-Zinn (1990) called "full-catastrophe living." That is the aim of this book.

The chapters of this workbook are organized around the eleven most problematic coping mechanisms that cause emotional pain. Each chapter starts with processes to reduce reliance on that mechanism, followed by positive change processes to do the opposite of your old coping behaviors.

How Does Process-Based CBT Work?

Emotional disorders start with moments of emotional pain. Emily is an example. She hated feeling anxious, but her demanding boss, her irritable boyfriend, and her critical family seemed to conspire to keep her chronically afraid. The truth is that these relationships weren't what kept Emily anxious. Rather, it was her negative coping mechanisms, such as:

- *Worry.* Emily worried about her boss disapproving of her performance, her boyfriend leaving her, and her family rejecting her for not being supportive enough. Worrying about rejection and disapproval only makes anxiety worse.

- *Emotion avoidance.* Every time Emily felt anxiety in her body, she tried to get rid of it. But all the efforts to suppress and control her feelings seemed to make them worse.

- *Safety seeking.* Emily procrastinated on deadlines at work and avoided her boss. She avoided talking to her mother, who always seemed so critical. And she alternated between withdrawing from her boyfriend and seeking reassurance that he still loves her. The more safety seeking and avoidance she did, the more anxious she seemed to feel.

- *Negative thinking.* Emily focused on the negative regarding nearly everything she did: a small mistake on a report she wrote, her boyfriend's serious expression as they ate dinner together, her mother not saying "I love you" at the end of a conversation. Small things added up to a sense that she was failing, and her anxiety went through the roof.

Through process-based CBT, Emily has learned to target her negative coping mechanisms with specific change processes.

For worry, she's learned *thought defusion* (watching and letting go of thoughts), *balanced thinking* using mindful meditation, and *attention switching* (from worry thoughts to what she can see, hear, smell, and touch).

For emotion avoidance, she's learned to *mindfully observe* her emotions (including sensations, thoughts, feelings, and urges) and practice the change process of *emotion exposure* (watching and allowing feelings of anxiety until they lose the power to scare her). She's also been practicing an *acceptance meditation* to learn how to accept and tolerate anxious feelings and sensations.

For safety seeking, she's learned the change process of *response prevention* (gradually reducing and then discontinuing all avoidance behavior).

And finally, for negative thinking, she's learned to use the change process of *flexible thinking* (analyzing a problem, generating possible solutions, evaluating and testing each solution, and, finally, acting on the best solution).

Using these positive change processes, Emily has greatly reduced her anxiety because she has learned *not* to use the old, anxiety-maintaining mechanisms.

How to Use This Book

Read the upcoming assessment chapter and take the self-assessment test. It will reveal which negative coping mechanisms you use most and are likely causing your emotional pain. Your scores on this test will be a map for using the rest of the book.

You will pick two or three mechanisms you scored the *highest* on and go first to those chapters. The exercises there will give you practice in the healthy change processes you need to overcome old coping patterns and build new ways to deal with your feelings. Practice the skills in those chapters for several weeks before moving on to other chapters that may interest you. There is no need to read all the chapters.

How to Get the Most from This Book

This book is designed to help you take action and change how you relate to your emotions. It isn't enough merely to read about and understand change processes; you'll need to *do* the exercises to reduce your use of negative coping mechanisms and build positive strengths. Each chapter will show you how to replace old negative coping mechanisms with healthy, effective ways to live. To get the most from the book, engage with and *do* the change processes. See which ones work best for you and integrate them into your daily life.

Many of the worksheets in the book are also available as free tools at http://www.newharbinger. com/50218. (See the very back of this book for more details.) We recommend downloading and printing these tools for future use to maintain your growth.

Where Did These Ideas Come From?

The ideas, interventions, and processes in this book were selected by the authors from a long legacy of thinkers and researchers. These processes are not new, and some of them have deep roots in Buddhist and other mindful traditions around the world. Most of the processes are adaptations and variations of treatments laid out in previous psychological literature, especially acceptance and commitment therapy, dialectical behavior therapy, and other forms of cognitive behavioral therapy, which are all evidence-based therapy interventions for individuals suffering from emotional disorders.

Ultimately, this book is written from a personal space, the perspective of four individuals who have four specific life experiences and education in the field of psychology in the United States. There are many, many ways to address pain, suffering, healing, and coping, and this perspective is not the only one that is valid or useful. That said, if you think that process-based CBT might be helpful for you, you'll have the opportunity here to dive in deeper with the potential to change your life.

When and How to Get More Help

Learning to change old habits is difficult for the human mind. The negative coping mechanisms described in the self-assessment are all very common, understandable responses to stress, and no human on this earth can ever be perfect at responding to pain. The overarching attitude in this book is one of acceptance: truly accepting that life will always include struggle and that by opening yourself up to struggle you can enjoy the richness of life.

You might encounter barriers to implementing the tools in this book, particularly if you're under a lot of stress from factors outside your control, such as a chronic illness, an imbalance in your neurochemistry, or large-scale social pressures. These are times to recruit extra help for your struggle. Extra help can be on a spectrum from talking things over with family and friends, to using yoga or meditation apps, to finding support groups or other community resources, to meeting with a professional therapist, to consulting with a medical doctor for physiological interventions. Only you know what level of help you need. It's okay to shift in and out of needing extra support for your struggles over the course of your life.

This book should not be considered a replacement for mental health care. If you're experiencing emotional pain at a high intensity or frequency and it's negatively impacting your ability to eat, sleep, connect with others, or take care of yourself, you may need much more support than can be offered through a book. You may wish to search on Google or *PsychologyToday.com* for a practitioner with a PhD, PsyD, MFT, LCSW, or MSW degree in your state and reach out. If you have health insurance, your insurer may cover mental health services.

If you're having thoughts of harming yourself or others, please reach out to crisis support. The Suicide Prevention Lifeline is 1-800-273-8255, and their website, suicidepreventionlifeline.org, has helpful resources. Your state or city may also have local crisis support lines; a quick Google search should reveal them.

What's Important: How You Respond to Emotional Pain

Emotional pain is inevitable. It shows up at different points and moments of life. Quite often this pain is initially out of your control. All you can control is how you *respond* to painful situations and feelings. You can cope in ways that make them worse, or you can use change processes to face and ultimately heal the pain. You can control how much energy you give to the pain, how much your life becomes about coping with it, and how much space you carve out to support yourself in the face of pain. This book is about how you want to respond and show up in your life, even when things hurt.

Comprehensive Coping Inventory–55

How do you cope with stress? What are you most likely to do when you're scared, anxious, depressed, ashamed, or angry? Do you run away, hide, or attack? Do you distract yourself or try not to think about what's bothering you? Do you ask for help, seek more information, or just endure a challenging experience until it's over?

There are many coping mechanisms for handling life's stressful experiences and painful emotions. Some work better than others. Some work very poorly. Some make the situation worse by prolonging your upset.

This Comprehensive Coping Inventory–55 (CCI-55; Zurita Ona 2007; Pool 2021) is the heart of the book. It is a simple test with a large research history that will indicate which of your coping mechanisms are not working for you. See the appendix for more information about the CCI-55.

Let's get started.

Instructions

Take this assessment all in one sitting. You can use the version printed here, or go to http://www.newharbinger.com/50218 and work online.

Be as honest as you possibly can. You are the only person who will see this, and you need to clearly see the areas where you're stuck. The ineffective coping mechanisms in the inventory are very common human experiences, based on a survey of thousands of ordinary people. There is no need to feel embarrassed if you realize you engage in some of these behaviors.

Think about difficult, upsetting, or stressful situations in your life in the past three months. Listed below are descriptions of common experiences and strategies for handling difficulty and stress. Please rate each item in terms of **how frequently** you experience it or **how frequently** you use that strategy.

Choose the most accurate answer for you, not what you think is the most acceptable or what most people would say or do. None of these are "good" or "bad." They are just different ways humans cope.

Rate each item on a scale from 1 to 5:

1 = I *almost never* have this experience or use this strategy.

2 = I *seldom* or rarely have this experience or use this strategy.

3 = I *sometimes* have this experience or use this strategy.

4 = I *often* have this experience or use this strategy.

5 = I *very often* have this experience or use this strategy.

	Item	Rate 1–5 *1 = Almost never* *5 = Very often*
Section 1		
1.1	When activities feel like "too much," I just don't do them, even if it means I miss out.	
2.1	I avoid things that make me feel upset.	
3.1	When I feel bad, I withdraw and avoid activities or tasks.	
4.1	When situations feel overwhelming, I just stay away from them.	
5.1	When activities seem too stressful or challenging, I find a reason not to do them.	
	Section 1 Total	
Section 2		
1.2	If I feel stressed or scared, I avoid situations altogether so I can feel safe – even though I wish I didn't have to.	
2.2	When I'm feeling anxious or upset, I have to get reassurance in order to feel that things will be okay.	
3.2	I repeatedly review and check things to feel reassured and reduce my anxiety.	

	Item	Rate 1–5 *1 = Almost never* *5 = Very often*
4.2	When I'm feeling worried or scared, there are very specific things I have to do to feel safe that others do not.	
5.2	In situations that make me worried, I use unique rituals or routines to try to alleviate my fears.	
	Section 2 Total	

Section 3

1.3	I often act on my emotions without thinking; I tend to do what they push me to do.	
2.3	If I feel strong negative emotions, I can feel driven to drink, use drugs, and/or cut or hurt myself in some way.	
3.3	When I'm upset, my behavior gets out of control.	
4.3	My emotions drive my behavior, even if it means I regret it after.	
5.3	If I feel strong emotions (such as shame or anger), I act in ways that hurt me or get me in trouble.	
	Section 3 Total	

Section 4

1.4	When I feel distressed or upset, I think to myself that I'd do anything to make it stop.	
2.4	Feeling distressed or very upset is intolerable to me.	
3.4	The experiences of distress (heart racing, scattered thoughts, tightness, tingling, etc.) are unbearable to me, and I'd do anything to avoid or get rid of them.	
4.4	When I feel the physical sensations of being distressed, I feel like I have to get rid of them right away.	

	Item	Rate 1–5 *1 = Almost never 5 = Very often*
5.4	The physical feelings of distress (racing heart, stomach clenching, choppy breath, etc.) feel dangerous or completely intolerable to me.	
	Section 4 Total	
Section 5		
1.5	I try to avoid or blank out my emotions when I'm upset.	
2.5	I usually try to push painful feelings away.	
3.5	I try to numb or shut off my negative feelings.	
4.5	There are some strong emotions (such as shame, anger, or sadness) that I try to avoid completely.	
5.5	When I'm upset, I try to fix my negative emotions, or make myself stop feeling them.	
	Section 5 Total	
Section 6		
1.6	When I have scary or upsetting thoughts, I immediately try to get rid of them.	
2.6	I push away memories and thoughts that bother me.	
3.6	I try to avoid or stop thinking about things that make me sad or anxious.	
4.6	It's important for me to block out painful thoughts.	
5.6	I try to avoid painful thoughts about bad things from the past.	
	Section 6 Total	

	Item	Rate 1–5 *1 = Almost never* *5 = Very often*
Section 7		
1.7	When situations are especially upsetting to me, I tend to have a string of thoughts about myself or others that feel true at the time, but often aren't.	
2.7	I easily jump to conclusions when I'm upset by something—and my conclusions aren't usually accurate.	
3.7	When I'm struggling, I tend to have all-or-nothing thoughts. (For example, "If I don't do this perfectly, it's worthless" or "They either love me, or they hate me.")	
4.7	When I'm in distress, I jump to conclusions very quickly.	
5.7	In difficult situations, I assume I know what other people are thinking or what is going to happen.	
	Section 7 Total	
Section 8		
1.8	I blame myself for things that go wrong.	
2.8	I judge myself and/or feel ashamed for my faults and mistakes.	
3.8	I criticize myself for decisions and choices I have made.	
4.8	When things go wrong, I assume it's my fault and try to pinpoint the mistake I made.	
5.8	I blame myself for things that other people don't think are my fault.	
	Section 8 Total	

	Item	Rate 1–5 1 = Almost never 5 = Very often
Section 9		
1.9	I judge the ways others handle things and get angry about it.	
2.9	I criticize others for their mistakes and faults.	
3.9	I notice and get angry when people don't act how I think they should.	
4.9	I find that when things go wrong for me, it's usually someone else's fault.	
5.9	When I'm solving a problem, I usually find that someone else has made a mistake or made me upset in some way.	
	Section 9 Total	
Section 10		
1.10	I think about all the bad things that could happen in the future.	
2.10	Wherever there's a problem, I tend to dwell on the worst things that could happen.	
3.10	I find that I tend to overthink bad scenarios that could happen.	
4.10	My problems trigger a lot of thinking about all the bad directions things could take.	
5.10	Whenever I have a problem, I spend a lot of time thinking about what I should do, and all the ways it could go wrong.	
	Section 10 Total	

	Item	Rate 1–5 1 = Almost never 5 = Very often
Section 11		
1.11	I dwell on troubling events in the past.	
2.11	I get lost in thoughts trying to understand or analyze why things happened the way they did.	
3.11	I keep thinking about, reliving, or trying to understand things in the past that upset me.	
4.11	When I have regrets about things in the past, I tend to think about them over and over.	
5.11	My mind often jumps to past events, and I get stuck trying to analyze them.	
	Section 11 Total	

Scoring

Now, you will need to do a little addition and subtraction.

Step 1

Add up the scores of each section (e.g., section 1, section 2). For example, in section 1, if you answered the following…

1.1	When activities feel like "too much," I just don't do them, even if it means I miss out.	3
2.1	I avoid things that make me feel upset.	4
3.1	When I feel bad, I withdraw and avoid activities or tasks.	4
4.1	When situations feel overwhelming, I just stay away from them.	3
5.1	When activities seem too stressful or challenging, I find a reason not to do them.	4

…the total for section 1, "Behavioral Avoidance," would be 18.

Step 2

Put each of your totals for all eleven sections in the "Your Score" column in the table below. Subtract the number shown in the "Subtract" column from your score. It's okay if you go into the negatives.

For example, if you scored 18 in the "Behavioral Avoidance" section, you'd subtract 14, and your final score in that section would be 4. If you scored 8 for "Safety Seeking," you'd subtract 13, and your final score would be -5.

You can use the blank form below to find all eleven of your final scores.

Section Number	Ineffective Coping Mechanism	Your Score	Subtract	Your Final Score	Change Process Chapter
1	Behavioral Avoidance		14		1 Engagement
2	Safety Seeking		13		2 Courage
3	Emotion-Driven Behavior		10		3 Passion
4	Distress Intolerance		13		4 Resilience
5	Emotion Avoidance		15		5 Openness
6	Thought Avoidance		16		6 Peace
7	Cognitive Misappraisals		12		7 Clarity
8	Self-Blame		13		8 Self-Esteem
9	Blaming Others		11		9 Patience
10	Worry		13		10 Serenity
11	Rumination		13		10 Serenity

How to Interpret Your Results

Look at each of your final scores and see which two or three areas are *highest* for you. Those are the chapters you'll want to read and practice first. Pick which chapter to start with by considering your highest score and which change processes seem most applicable to you at this time.

When you have learned the skills taught in your first chapter and are becoming successful with choosing more effective ways of dealing with stress and your painful feelings, return here to remind yourself of the next area you'd like to work on.

For the Long Term: After you have worked your way through two or three chapters, you should be well on your way to using more effective change processes. However, sometimes stress levels rise and you may find yourself falling into older bad habits, using your less effective coping mechanisms more frequently. So before you close this book for the last time and put it on your shelf, check out the last chapter, "Relapse Prevention."

CHAPTER 1

Engagement: From Behavioral Avoidance to Action

You have turned to this chapter because you scored high on section 1 of the Comprehensive Coping Inventory–55, "Behavioral Avoidance." That means you avoid situations and activities that make you feel nervous, afraid, guilty, ashamed, or like a failure. When you make a habit of avoiding the situations and activities that bring up these emotions, and the avoidance becomes too strong and enduring, it can result in chronic depression. This chapter will help you recognize and change avoidance behaviors that have been keeping you sad and stuck and will show you how to get mobilized so you can get unstuck, stop disconnecting, and get back to your life.

Behavioral Avoidance: What It Is

As a species, we are hardwired to avoid, control, and escape whatever makes us uncomfortable. That's natural and expected. In other words, to avoid is to be human. But what happens when we avoid things that we care about because they make us uncomfortable or sad? What happens when we disconnect from the things that matter to us because we're trying to control what we feel? What's the long-term outcome of avoidant behaviors in our lives?

Example. To illustrate behavioral avoidance and its effects, let's consider Justin's situation. When Justin was twenty-one years old, he got his first job working as a manager for a local restaurant. He was more than excited about his job, his paycheck, and the possibilities of expanding his career in the food industry. After a couple of months of working, he returned home on a Friday evening and saw his dog of fourteen years, Jackson, lying on the floor. Justin got scared and tried to move Jackson, but Jackson didn't respond. Justin immediately took his dog to the veterinarian. In less than an hour, Justin was told that Jackson had had a heart attack and was dead. Justin couldn't make sense of those words. He drove mechanically back home and cried for hours.

Every night after work Justin felt sad, empty, as if something was missing. His friends tried to get him to go out, his family reached out too, but nothing diminished Justin's grief. Little by little, Justin became disconnected from his friends. He called in sick to work some days, and the idea of moving on and getting a new puppy felt strange to him. Justin felt responsible for Jackson's passing away. He blamed himself for not catching the early signs of a heart attack. He slowly withdrew from everyone, the things he needed to do, and the things he cared about.

Justin is struggling with behavioral avoidance, the leading cause of depression. What started as a painful loss grew into deactivation and disengagement from life. Behavioral avoidance is characterized by withdrawal from activities you value, enjoy, or must do to make life work. The other side of avoidance is engagement: doing what matters with appreciation and gratitude.

Processes That Reduce Behavioral Avoidance

By assessing your day-to-day life, determining what you're avoiding, and understanding and identifying your values, you can get back to doing the things you used to enjoy or start doing what you have always wanted to try. And in the process overcome depression. Let's get started.

Assessing How You're Spending Your Time

As a starting point, it's important that you assess how you're spending your time. So, over the next week, using the weekly calendar below, record all the main activities you participate in each hour; it's okay if you jot them down at the end of the day.

When monitoring your activities, pay attention to the following aspects:

- If an activity was pleasurable, fun, or enjoyable, write a letter "P" for pleasurable next to it; next, rank it from 1 (minimum) to 10 (maximum) in terms of how much fun it was.

- If an activity is related to your values and what's important to you, write a letter "V" for values next to it; then, rank it from 1 (minimum) to 10 (maximum) in terms of how important to you it was.

- If an activity is related to things you need to take care off (for example, errands, paying bills, cleaning), write a letter "M" for must-do next to it; also rank it from 1 (minimum) to 10 (maximum) in terms of how much of a priority it is to get it done.

This may seem a bit tedious at the beginning. However, completing the assessment will help you recognize how your week looks currently, how it's impacting your well-being, and what needs to change so you can break any avoidance patterns. Think about it: if you don't know how you're spending your time, you won't know what you need to change.

As a reminder, this worksheet, and all others in this book, can also be found at http://www.newharbinger.com/50218.

Weekly Activity Schedule

	Mon.	Tues.	Wed.	Thurs.	Fri.	Sat.	Sun.
6 a.m.							
7 a.m.							
8 a.m.							
9 a.m.							
10 a.m.							
11 a.m.							
12 noon							
1 p.m.							
2 p.m.							
3 p.m.							
4 p.m.							
5 p.m.							
6 p.m.							
7 p.m.							
8 p.m.							
9 p.m.							
10 p.m.							
11 p.m.							
12–6 a.m.							

Example. When Mohammed reviewed his activity schedule at the end of the week, he realized that he spent more than thirty hours watching TV, even though he didn't enjoy it; he spent almost twelve hours dealing with tax problems without a break; and he had barely any social interaction with his children and friends, which was something very important for him.

Mohammed's Weekly Activity Schedule

	Mon.	Tues.	Wed.	Thurs.	Fri.	Sat.	Sun.
6 a.m.							
7 a.m.							
8 a.m.					Reviewing taxes		
9 a.m.	Calling IRS				Reviewing taxes	Working	
10 a.m.	Reviewing taxes	Working	Working	Working	Reviewing taxes	Working	
11 a.m.	Reviewing taxes	Working	Working	Working	Reviewing taxes	Working	TV
12 noon	Reviewing taxes	Working	Working	Working	Calling IRS	Working	TV
1 p.m.	Calling IRS	Working	Working	Working		Working	TV
2 p.m.	Reviewing taxes	Working	Working	Working		Working	TV
3 p.m.	Reviewing taxes	Working	Working	Working		Working	TV
4 p.m.	TV			TV		Working	TV
5 p.m.	TV			TV		Working	TV
6 p.m.	TV			TV		Working	TV
7 p.m.	TV			TV	TV	TV	TV
8 p.m.	TV			TV	TV	TV	
9 p.m.	TV			TV	TV	TV	
10 p.m.	TV			TV	TV	TV	
11 p.m.							
12–6 a.m.							

Determining What You're Avoiding

Take a few minutes to do an inventory of the things you have disconnected from during the recent months; don't worry how long or short the list is, just write down all the things you have been avoiding up to this point.

Avoidance Inventory

Activities, Situations, and People You Avoided	Short-Term Consequences	Long-Term Consequences

After identifying all the situations you have withdrawn from, take a look at the consequences of those actions in your day-to-day life and over the short and long term. Below is an example.

Activities, Situations, and People You Avoided	Short-Term Consequences	Long-Term Consequences
Example: Taking calls from my friends	Don't get stressed about talking to people Don't have to answer questions about how I'm feeling	Miss connecting, socializing with the people who matter to me Feel more sad, alone

Withdrawing behaviors are tricky because they feel comfortable in the short term and they can help you feel safe. In the long term, when left unchecked, they can take you away from doing what's important, from the people you love, and from the things you need to do. Whether you're avoiding situations sporadically or chronically, this chapter will help you disrupt those avoidance patterns and reset your actions toward what you care about.

Your best line of defense is to step back from this avoidance dance and reconnect with your values, the things you find fun, and the things you need to do.

Understanding Values

Values have been the source of inspiration for artists, creators, leaders, and almost every single person on earth who wants to live with meaning, purpose, and intention.

"Values" means different things to different people. For the purposes of this workbook, think of values as the response to these key questions: *Are you living the life you want to live? What sort of person do you want to be? Are you the family member you want to be? Are you doing what matters to you as a friend? Are you treating yourself the way you really, deeply want in your heart?*

In a nutshell, according to acceptance and commitment therapy, values are the deepest desires, wishes, qualities, and life principles you want to live by. Your values—like a life compass—point you toward the path you want your life to take. They give you inspiration, motivation, vitality, and a strong sense of fulfillment.

Before diving into figuring out your values, here are things to consider:

Values versus goals. Values are the "why" of what you do, and they're different from goals. Goals are specific stepping-stones along the path leading you in the direction of your values. Goals are actions that you complete and check off a list. For instance, Rebecca, as a mother, identifies her value as "being caring," while some of her goals are to (1) prepare lunch for her daughter every day, (2) drive her daughter to gymnastics twice a week, and (3) check in about her daughter's experience on school days. In essence, Rebecca sets her goals and actions in line with her values; her actions may change, but her values don't.

Values are not feelings. Feeling good does not mean you're living your values. And values are not about feeling good. In fact, living your values and doing what matters comes with uncomfortable feelings at times. For instance, for Joe, being caring with his relatives is a core value; every month he travels for six hours to spend a day with his ninety-year-old grandmother, who cannot travel, barely recognizes him, and requires assistance at all times. As soon as he arrives, Joe grooms her, reads her a favorite book, and leaves pictures of her great-grandchildren. Even when she calls him by the wrong name, he holds her hand. Joe feels sad and frustrated, and he believes it's unfair that a woman who raised nine children struggles to remember them. Yet even though performing these actions in service of his values makes him uncomfortable, he continues to visit.

Values are not about avoiding feelings. If your mind says that the outcome you want in life is to feel less pain, to have less intense and fewer stressful emotions like anxiety or sadness, it's understandable. But avoiding feelings, as previously noted, only makes the pain worse. Not only will you face significant depression, but a life of avoidance rather than values devitalizes you. You may begin to feel that life has no point or purpose.

Values are not your preferences. There are things that we like, love, and go out of our way to get. For instance, you may love your morning coffee, a sunny day on the beach, or salsa dancing; all those things are fun, and you may want to have a lot of those moments, but those are preferences, not values. Your morning coffee, as tasty as it is, isn't pointing you in the direction of doing what matters to you; your values do that. Your values are like the arrow on a compass that points the way for you to go.

Values are not your wishes for others' behaviors. Sometimes, when having a conversation about values, people will say, "I want to be respected by others." It's natural to want to be seen, appreciated, and respected by others, and you certainly deserve it. But here is the takeaway: you simply do not have control of other people's reactions, behaviors, and feelings about you. Values-based actions are about your *own* behavior and choices.

Living your values is an actionable task. Taking steps toward what matters to you gives you a new way of being in the world; It's not pain-free, but it means you get to choose how you want to live your life, instead of your emotions choosing for you and dragging you around in the process. The more steps you take toward becoming the person you want to be, the better life gets—and as they say, "What you practice, grows." The next section of this chapter will help you to clarify the things that matter to you and how you can take steps toward them.

Identifying Your Values

Below is a two-part exercise that you can use as a guide to identify your values; we encourage you to do both parts since they're complementary.

Exercise 1: What Are My Values?

Part 1. On the worksheet below, write about three different moments when you had a sense of vitality and felt alive, when you were doing what speaks deeply to you, when in that moment life was just perfect. Describe each situation, the person you were with, and what you were doing. Imagine that someone was recording you in those moments—what would they see in the camera?

After recalling and writing about these three different memories, try to identify any qualities that stand out to you across all of them. Ask yourself: *What was special for me about those moments? How did I feel about myself? What was the quality or way of being I was embracing that made me feel good in those moments?*

Your answers will point you to your values. On the bottom of the worksheet, jot down the values you came up with, keeping in mind that your values are verbs. You don't need to have a shopping list of your values, just a refined list of what you strive to be and stand for in your personal life. As a reference, you can look at this list of values:

Saying what you think	Being accepting	Belonging
Being creative	Learning	Being real
Connecting	Being silly	Forgiving
Caring	Being humble	Knowing
Being healthy	Understanding others	Being open
Having freedom	Being curious	Discovering

Don't worry about finding the perfect word or the perfect value, just list the principles that you want to embrace in your life and be remembered for by others. The purpose of this exercise is not to identify the perfect value but to get in touch with what truly matters to you.

Identifying Your Values Worksheet

Describe three different memories of times when you had a sense of vitality, felt alive, and were doing what speaks deeply to you.

My values are…

Example. After completing this exercise, Anne came up with the following memories:

Describe three different memories of times when you had a sense of vitality, felt alive, and were doing what speaks deeply to you.

Memory 1: When celebrating my daughter's sixth birthday, I looked at her and felt a strong sense of connection with her and felt how much I wanted to be a constant part of her life in a way that she knows I love her.

Memory 2: On a rainy day, my partner and I were struggling to figure out what to do to entertain ourselves. We flipped channels and didn't see anything interesting. We thought about eating, but nothing seemed exciting. We decided to walk our dog in our neighborhood and, to my surprise, that was one of the sweetest moments we had. It was cold, we were wearing our heavy jackets, but when walking together we remembered the first home we had, how hard we worked for it, how we decorated it, how much we argued about the tile in the bathroom, and how we couldn't stop smiling when thinking of the bright yellow door we painted in the kitchen. I felt so clear about not needing extravagant or fancy things all the time to enjoy myself and my husband's company.

Memory 3: I remember a tough conversation I needed to have at work with my sister, who was also my manager, about a salary raise. I couldn't sleep for days, felt anxious, and asked for advice from any person I could find. In the past, no matter what I asked for, whether it was for something at work, at home, or anywhere, my sister would usually say no.

I prepared a draft of what I was going to tell my sister and rehearsed in front of a mirror. I even had a back-up plan if she didn't raise my salary. On the day of our meeting, I had my coffee, wore my favorite sweater, and then walked to her office. She greeted me warmly and then asked about my request for revising my salary. I felt my body get sweaty all over, and I felt a rush, like I wanted to run away, but I stayed and told her that I needed a raise and recited the reasons why. My sister looked at me, didn't say much while I was talking, and after nodding her head, said that she would think about it and discuss it. She wanted me to know that no one in my department had received a raise in the last six months. For the first time, I didn't walk away from a conflict and didn't apologize for asking for what I needed. And even though I didn't get the raise immediately but instead two months later, I knew I did the right thing for myself.

My values are…

Being caring, down to earth, and authentic.

Part 2. Imagine that you have lived your life the best you could up to this point. Some things have gone as you wanted them to go, and some have been difficult. Some things you planned, and others just happened. Here you are today, living your life, when things suddenly take a dramatic new course for you: Right now, in this moment, you're being notified that you're going to die in the next twenty-four hours. Suddenly you realize you only have a short amount of time to be alive and prepare for your final departure. You may start breathing fast. You might ask yourself, *Given how things are right now, what type of person do I want to be?* You're living your last day on earth. You're running out of time. There is no turning back. This is it. Please reflect on this and contemplate it a moment. Then, knowing what you know now, complete the same worksheet as in Part 1, with either the same or different memories.

Identifying Your Values Worksheet

Describe three different past memories when you had a sense of vitality, felt alive, and were doing what speaks deeply to you.

My values are…

Identifying the moments in your life that are most meaningful to you and contemplating your mortality—as difficult as that may be—helps you to identify what truly matters to you. Now let's move on to acknowledging the life areas that you care about.

Exercise 2: What Areas Are Important to Me?

People tend to have strong values in eight general areas of life (Hayes and Smith 2005). Some of these areas will be more important to you than others. Read through the following descriptions of these domains and circle four that are most important to you.

Intimate relationships. What kind of partner do you want to be to your significant other?

Parenting. What is most important to you about parenting your kids?

Friends and social life. How do you want to show up for your friends?

Health. What's important to you when you think about your health?

Family relationships. What is most important about your relationships with your parents, siblings, children, or other family members?

Spirituality or religion. What are your spiritual values? Why are you here in this life? How are you connected to the universe?

Community life and citizenship. How do you want to show up to others in your community?

Work and career. What are the qualities you want to embrace at work and in your career?

Now that you have a sense of your values and the areas of your life that are important to you, write down the four areas (and respective values) you want to focus on and commit to as you move forward.

Values Commitment Worksheet

The areas and values that I commit to work on are:

    Area:

    Value:

    Area:

    Value:

    Area:

    Value:

    Area:

    Value:

Anne's completed worksheet looked like this:

The areas and values that I commit to work on are:

    Area: Career

    Value: Disseminating research—based skills to the lay audience

    Area: Romantic relationships

    Value: Being present and caring; connecting

    Area: Spirituality

    Value: Being grateful

    Area: Health

    Value: Balancing career, relationships, health, and spiritual life

---

You will be coming back to Anne and this exercise later in the chapter, so be sure to earmark it so you can return to it then.

Here's an important thing to keep in mind about values: words about values without any action are like beautiful leaves swept away by the wind. You don't want your values blown away. So let's move into identifying specific change processes you can engage in to live those values.

Processes That Increase Action

We've covered the processes necessary to reduce behavioral avoidance and are ready to focus on activation, or increasing action. In this section, we'll cover the three major change processes that are effective at replacing life-restricting patterns with action:

- **Values-based activation,** which comes from acceptance and commitment therapy (ACT) and establishes that committing to values-based behavior improves your motivation and willingness to overcome experiential avoidance (Zettle 2007)

- **Behavioral activation,** which involves making changes by increasing activity, counteracting avoidant behaviors, and increasing access to positive reinforcers (Hopko et al. 2003)

- **Activity scheduling**, which was initially developed to overcome depression (Beck et al. 1979; Freeman et al. 2004; Greenberger and Padesky 1995)

You'll also learn ways to identify and overcome potential roadblocks to action and augment your engagement with life.

Identifying Actions to Align with Your Values (Values-Based Activation)

You cannot explore New York by driving the streets of Seattle. In the same way, you cannot live your values by taking actions in random, unrelated directions. Rather, you must intentionally choose specific actions, steps, and goals you need to take in the right direction.

It's time to identify specific actions that will bring your life into closer alignment with your key values. When thinking of actions and goals, keep in mind the following principles:

- Goals and actions must be concrete and achievable, given your circumstances.

- Goals and actions must be specific, answering who, why, how, where, and for how long.

You can use the following worksheet to aid in this process. As a starting point, choose any four areas of life from the list in Exercise 2. In the first column, write the area you want to focus on. In the next column, write at least three values for each area. And in the last column, think of and write down a specific action you can do that reflects each key value.

Values-Based Activities Worksheet

Area	Value	Values-Based Activity

Example. Here's how Roland completed this worksheet.

Area	Value	Values-Based Activity
Intimate relationships	Connecting	Invite my partner for a weekly breakfast every Friday morning.
	Being present	Ask my partner about the challenging situation she's dealing at work and intentionally listen to the difficulties she's experiencing.
	Being supportive	On Saturday morning, take my partner's car to the mechanic for maintenance.

Getting Mobilized for Action (Behavioral Activation)

Now that you've identified some values-based actions you can take, let's explore some strategies to propel you to action.

Get mobilized with fun and pleasurable activities. Withdrawing behaviors happen not only with the activities that are important to you, but also with things that are fun, enjoyable, and pleasurable. So, in this section, you are invited to select common, day-to-day, pleasurable activities to start participating in. If you have a hard time coming up with ideas, here is a list of popular ones for inspiration. Keep in mind that this list is a generic one, and you may want to add a more specific activity. For instance, if "exercising" is something you want to start doing again, try to narrow the activity to running, biking, or whatever you enjoy doing.

- Visiting friends or family
- Talking to friends or family on the phone
- Going to movies or plays
- Watching videos
- Exercising
- Playing games
- Chatting on the internet
- Listening to music
- Going away for a weekend
- Planning a vacation
- Pursuing a hobby
- Collecting items
- Doing crafts
- Enjoying the sun
- Walking or hiking
- Reading
- Gardening

If you are still struggling to come up with ideas, ask your friends and relatives for suggestions. Also, think back to the things you've enjoyed in the past. Try to remember everything you've ever done that was fun.

Now, take some time to jot down specific activities that you have enjoyed or can imagine enjoying in the future. Write down at least twelve.

Pleasurable Activities

1.

2.

3.

4.

5.

6.

7.

8.

9.

10.

11.

12.

13.

14.

15.

16.

17.

18.

19.

20.

Moving forward, let's take a look at all those errands, activities, and duties you have that can be hard to complete because you feel too depressed to do them. Let's break the cycle of inactivity and get you moving.

Getting mobilized with must-do activities. Our lives also include activities that must get done: paying bills, going to medical appointments, grocery shopping, and so forth. It's quite likely that you have disconnected from these activities too, and, as a result, you have a pile of postponed responsibilities that are causing you more distress.

Example. Isabella had accumulated what felt like a mountain of must-do activities she had been avoiding. She listed as many as she could think of:

Paying my cell phone bill

Completing my application for grad school

Applying for medical insurance

Searching for a temporary job (before I start grad school)

Scheduling a doctor's appointment

Doing groceries for this week

Calling my landlord

Taking my car to the mechanic

Buying a new pedestal for the TV

Getting a gift for my mom's birthday

Fixing the leg of the night table

Getting a frame for my family picture

Now do an inventory of your must-do activities. Write down at least twelve.

Must-Do Activities I Need to Take Care Of

1.

2.

3.

4.

5.

6.

7.

8.

9.

10.

11.

12.

13.

14.

15.

16.

17.

18.

19.

20.

Building your weekly calendar. Now that you have identified your values—along with values-based actions, fun activities, and must-do tasks—let's schedule them. You may wonder, *Why do I have to schedule them if I know what I need to do?* A simple reason: tracking what you do and how you spend your time keeps you accountable and motivates you to keep moving.

So, here is what you need to do:

- Grab a pen and the Weekly Activity Schedule below. For each day of the week, do the following:

  - Go back to the Values-Based Activities Worksheet and schedule one values-based activity. Next to it, enter a letter "V" for values.

  - Go back to the Pleasurable Activities Worksheet and schedule one of those activities. Next to it, enter the letter "P" for pleasure.

  - Go back to the Must-Do Activities I Need To Take Care Of worksheet and schedule one of them. Next to it, enter the letter "M" for must-do.

You'll begin by scheduling one activity per day from each category, but you can increase and change them in succeeding weeks.

Weekly Activity Schedule

	Mon.	Tues.	Wed.	Thurs.	Fri.	Sat.	Sun.
6 a.m.							
7 a.m.							
8 a.m.							
9 a.m.							
10 a.m.							
11 a.m.							
12 noon							
1 p.m.							
2 p.m.							

	Mon.	Tues.	Wed.	Thurs.	Fri.	Sat.	Sun.
3 p.m.							
4 p.m.							
5 p.m.							
6 p.m.							
7 p.m.							
8 p.m.							
9 p.m.							
10 p.m.							
11 p.m.							
12–6 a.m.							

Here is how Isabella completed her Weekly Activity Schedule:

	Mon.	Tues.	Wed.	Thurs.	Fri.	Sat.	Sun.
6 a.m.							
7 a.m.				Going for a bike ride (V)			
8 a.m.	Completing my application for grad school (M)		Going for a hike (P)		Paying my cell phone bill (M)	Journaling (V)	
9 a.m.							Doing groceries for this week (M)
10 a.m.		Searching for a temporary job (before I start grad school) (M)					
11 a.m.							
12 noon	Making a pizza (P)			Applying for medical insurance (M)			Enjoying the sun (P)
1 p.m.		Taking my car to the mechanic (M)				Calling my landlord (M)	
2 p.m.			Exercising (V)		Calling my parents (V)		

3 p.m.						Buying a new pedestal for the TV (M)
4 p.m.						
5 p.m.	Scheduling a doctor's appointment (M)					
6 p.m.		Cooking a meal (V)		Putting together playlists for exercising, hiking, and riding my bike (P)			Preparing pizza from scratch (V)
7 p.m.	Listening to music (P)		Playing games (P)		Calling my high school mates (V)		
8 p.m.						
9 p.m.						
10 p.m.						
11 a.m.						
12–6 a.m.						

You now have your weekly calendar. That's a big step, but let's make sure you have the tools needed to commit to it.

Committing to Your Weekly Calendar (Activity Scheduling)

Committing to behavioral change improves your motivation and willingness to increase your activity levels and overcome different forms of avoidance (Hayes and Smith 2005). Keep in mind that committing to your weekly calendar is not about expecting a particular outcome; it's about committing to experience, allow, and stay with what comes with that decision. With every choice you make, there is an experience that comes as a result of the choice.

We encourage you to make commitments using the following tool:

For this particular activity: _____
(enter the activity)

I am willing to experience _____
(enter the type of discomfort you may experience)

So I can _____
(enter the benefits of implementing that particular action)

Isabella's commitment exercise looks like this:

For this particular activity: <u>completing my grad school application</u>

I am willing to experience <u>anxiety, self-doubt, and the urge to procrastinate</u>

So I can <u>move forward to accomplish my goal of attending grad school.</u>

If you put into action all these steps on a weekly basis, you will notice a shift in your day-to-day life. The key is acting on your values, taking care of the things you need to do, and having pleasurable activities on a daily basis. A rich life has multiple sources of engagement and pleasure, and this variability of experiences is key to breaking avoidance patterns and living the life you want to live.

Identifying and Overcoming Roadblocks

You've learned several skills to reduce behavioral avoidance and increase action, but it's important to anticipate potential roadblocks that may come your way as you do more and reengage with life. To unlearn avoidant behaviors and replace them with action, you will need to make room for difficult feelings, uncomfortable thoughts, and annoying sensations in your body. This may be very challenging for you, but the reward of living the life you want to live is worth it. List activities you wish to schedule in the next week (based on the Weekly Activity Schedule you completed above). Then note the roadblocks that you anticipate may show up—situations, thoughts, or feelings that might get in your way. Don't worry if they seem silly or stupid, just write them down so you can make an action plan for each one:

Identifying Potential Roadblocks

Type of Activity V= values M = must-do P = pleasure	Activity	Potential Roadblock

Remember Anne from earlier in the chapter? Anne identified these roadblocks:

Type of Activity V= values M = must-do P = pleasure	Activity	Potential Roadblock
M	Paying my bills	Will feel anxious when looking at the amounts
P	Reading Harry Potter novels	Difficulty concentrating; worry that I won't finish, like other things I start
V = Connecting	Inviting my partner for an evening check-in about what happened in our day	Boredom, tiredness, the possibility of conflict

Next, you will learn two specific ways to overcome your roadblocks:

1. **Visualization.** Choose one activity to work on, and visualize the steps required for this activity. Close your eyes and mentally walk yourself through all the steps you need to take to achieve your goal. Use all of your senses to experience each step as vividly as you can. Who are you with? What do you do or say? What are the circumstances? As you visualize the sequence of events in detail, note any thoughts, feelings, and sensations that might interfere with acting in accordance with your values and achieving your goal. As you notice your internal experiences, say to yourself, *Here is an emotion, here is a thought.* Do your best not to fight any of the internal experiences; simply acknowledge them as you continue visualizing the steps you need to take to complete that activity.

2. **Problem solving.** Create a problem-solving plan. Some of the activities you identified may seem big, painful, or undoable. To increase the likelihood of having your ideal outcome, you can develop a modified action (problem-solving) plan, which involves breaking things down into more manageable steps. Fill out the worksheet below; in the last section, try to break the activity down into at least three steps.

Modified Action Plan Worksheet

Type of activity:

Activity:

Roadblock:

The specific steps of my modified action plan are:

Let's look at Anne's roadblock and modified action plan for one of her values-based activities:

Type of activity: values

Activity: Inviting my partner for an evening check-in about what happened in our day.

Roadblock: Boredom, tiredness, the possibility of conflict

The specific steps of my modified action plan are:

- Ask my partner if they're interested each night.

- Check for a mutually agreed-upon time.

- Share a relaxing beverage or snack before starting.

As you can see, having a modified action plan makes things more manageable because you're breaking them down into micro-steps.

Notice what happens when you make an effort to establish a modified action plan for a potential roadblock or visualize the steps you need to take. Does the task feel more manageable? Do you feel more willingness to take it on?

After you have identified and surmounted these potential roadblocks, let's increase your willingness and motivation to make it happen. The next section will help you with that.

Augmenting Your Engagement with Life

Finally, in addition to the change processes we've covered to increase activation, there are two important ways to increase your engagement with life and your relationships: appreciation and gratitude.

Appreciation Skills

The term "appreciation" comes from two Latin words: *ad,* which means "toward," and *pretium,* which means "worth, value, price." Based on these roots, appreciation essentially means to see the value in other people's experiences, behaviors, responses, and wisdom. Appreciation nourishes relationships with others, cultivates your capacity to create stable and solid connections with others, and, consequently, improves your overall well-being.

You can incorporate appreciation skills in your daily activities by remembering the phrase "Let's NAP," which stands for three specific steps: Notice, Appreciate, and Praise verbally and immediately. You can remember these steps by using the simple acronym NAP.

Noticing is simply about seeing a specific behavior.

Appreciating is recognizing the value of the other person's behavior.

Praising is letting the other person know right away that you see the value in their behavior. Praising statements can start with "I like that you…," "I enjoy it when you…," "I appreciate that you…," or "It makes me smile when you…"

Over the next four weeks, commit to practicing your NAP skills every time you see a person doing something you value or something that you want to see happening more often, even though it may be a small behavior. You will be surprised by the effect that explicit appreciation can have on your relationships—and on your own engagement with life. What you appreciate, you emulate.

Gratitude Skills

Reflecting on what you feel grateful for in your day-to-day life lights up areas of your brain that are involved in regulating emotions. A simple gratitude practice makes you more resilient and fosters your capacity to handle overwhelming, stressful, and upsetting situations.

Gratitude doesn't mean you float through life in a state of bliss every time you do the laundry or look up at the sunset. It's more like a skill you practice to intentionally focus your thoughts on good things happening around you, even if they seem minor. By purposely choosing what to pay attention to, absorbing those moments, and noticing what feels good, you are regulating your attention and teaching your brain that no matter what noise is in the background, you can choose how to spend your time, energy, and effort.

For example, Yusun incorporated a gratitude practice by sending a thank-you text to her neighbor for watching her pets, thanking her husband for making a meal, telling herself how she appreciates the full mobility of her body during walks, and letting her best friend know how she enjoyed the lunch they had together a week ago.

Here are some suggestions for you to add to your weekly calendar:

- Start a gratitude journal.

- Write down a list of things you're grateful for at the end of the day.

- Write a gratitude letter to a person you appreciate.

- Create a gratitude box: once a week, take a moment to write down on a card what you're grateful for during your week and place it in a special box.

Gratitude skills can be rehearsed, practiced, and carried out just like any other behavior. You simply have to make the choice to do it. The rewards can be great: reduced depression and more engagement with things that feel good.

Summary

In this chapter you learned how to get mobilized—to stop struggling with avoidance, withdrawal, and disconnecting patterns—and how to augment your day-to-day activities to increase your sense of well-being.

Some days, putting these skills into action may be hard, but it gets easier if you make them part of your regular routine. Adding values-based, must do, and pleasurable activities to your weekly activity schedule on a regular basis will improve the quality of your life, make you more resilient, and increase your ability to handle the challenging moments that come your way—without avoiding, disconnecting, or withdrawing.

From here, return to the assessment chapter and look at your next highest scores on the Comprehensive Coping Inventory–55. That will tell you which chapter to work on next.

CHAPTER 2

Courage: From Safety Seeking to Inner Safety

Based on your responses to section 2 of the Comprehensive Coping Inventory–55, you may be relying too much, too quickly, and too often on habitual safety-seeking actions. Here are some everyday examples of how you might engage in safety-seeking actions:

- driving to a job site days before a job interview so you don't get lost on the day of the interview

- rehearsing a public presentation a dozen times so you don't make a fool of yourself when the moment comes

- thinking right away about something positive when having negative thoughts

- not telling your boss what you really think about a project so you don't create problems

- avoiding reading the news so you don't feel anxious about what's happening

This chapter will teach you how to recognize your safety-seeking actions, replace them with direct exposure to feared situations, and develop an inner sense of safety.

Safety Seeking: What It Is

We're emotional beings. Some of the emotions we experience are fun and exciting, and we can't wait to feel them again. Other emotions are hard to have; we dislike them, and at times we seek to control them. There is one type of emotion in particular that can drag us up and down, left and right: fear.

Our ancestors faced all types of dangerous situations: predators, perilous weather conditions, rivalries, hazardous topographies, hostility within social groups, banishment, unknown illnesses, and many other conditions that could spell death. All those pressures resulted in a hard-wired focus on threat and fear-based reactions: worries, anxieties, panic, obsessions, and many variations. As we evolved, humans learned to survive following the rule "better safe than sorry" and developed a complex set of behaviors to avoid threats—both internal threats like scary thoughts and external dangers.

The psychology literature refers to these behaviors as "safety-seeking behaviors, or safety behaviors," terms first coined by P. Salkovskis in 1996. Since then, as studies progressed, it has become clear that safety behaviors are present not only across all anxiety disorders but as a natural response for every human being when facing a perceived threat.

All those reactions are natural and not particularly problematic. However, as you'll see, many safety behaviors—such as checking, reassurance seeking, procrastination, overpreparing, and escape/avoidance—have the unintended consequence of making you more anxious and vulnerable to the uncertainties of life. The challenge with approaching all stressful situations with safety seeking is that your capacity to experience the uncertain, unpredictable, and imperfect situations that come your way becomes restricted. In other words, your ability to manage fearful situations is limited to safety crutches. When all you know how to do is to avoid uncertainty, uncertainty itself feels more and more intolerable and the world feels less and less safe.

It's not your fault that you learned to rely a lot on safety-seeking actions. Again, it's natural to do so because the purpose of safety behaviors is to avoid the discomfort, distress, and anxiety that arises when encountering an anxiety-triggering threat. All the safety-seeking behaviors are forms of avoidance, but some are more clear-cut than others.

Below we'll describe the six most common safety behaviors—distraction, overpreparing, procrastination, asking for reassurance, checking, and direct avoidance—so you can easily distinguish them, catch each one, and put into action some change processes to end or reduce them.

Distraction

Distraction is an attempt to avoid scary or obsessive thoughts. Many people who struggle with obsessive-compulsive disorder (OCD) have thoughts that disturb or scare them. These thoughts can include sexual images, the thought of doing or saying something that feels unacceptable, blasphemous thoughts, thoughts of harming other people (with no actual intention to do so), and countless others.

Distraction can work briefly, but the banished thought soon returns and brings with it another burst of fear. Dan, who struggles with OCD, frequently has the obsessive image of stabbing his girlfriend. He loves her and has no desire to hurt her, but the thought keeps showing up with a lot of fear and self-disgust. He distracts himself with plans to say and do nice things for her or with ritual phrases like "no, no, no" or "please let it stop," but then checks (see "Checking") to see if the images are there. And, sure enough, they are.

Procrastination

When relying on this form of safety-seeking behavior, you postpone a task on hand so you don't face the distress that comes with it. For instance, Pamela has to complete her thesis to graduate from business school. But every time she sits down to write it or thinks about doing it, she feels a strong sensation in her chest, her heart begins to beat fast, and she has thoughts like *I don't think I can do this. What if I don't pass?* Minutes later, she turns on the TV to watch her favorite show; other times, she starts making a meal or calls one of her friends as a way to avoid the discomfort that comes when thinking about working on her thesis.

Procrastinating behaviors have many variations, like rescheduling a meeting, distracting yourself with fun activities, delaying the delivery dates of projects, and many more. But all of these actions are done with the purpose of avoiding facing anxiety about a particular project.

Overpreparing

These are behaviors you do to make sure you don't make a mistake, fail, or make a fool of yourself. But they aren't helpful when you take it to the extreme. For example, Peter, a journalist, is preparing to give a talk. He writes three different outlines, rehearses each one of them multiple times, records himself, watches the videos, and asks his friends to watch them. But after all of that, he still doesn't think that his talk is good enough, so he considers writing a fourth draft.

Reassurance Seeking

Asking for reassurance plays out in actions you do to remove any sense of uncertainty when facing a new task, project, situation, or activity. Let's think of Natasha, a thirty-three-year-old transgender person who asks to be referred to as "they." When Natasha goes on a date, after having a conversation with a potential partner, they go home full of concern about whether the other person liked them or not, what the date thought about them, and whether the date will contact them again or not. Usually on their way back home, Natasha quickly sends a text asking the other person, "Are we cool? Did we connect?" Despite acknowledging feedback in the past that maybe they were trying to force reactions too soon, Natasha keeps doing the same old behaviors, all driven by this intense fear of not knowing.

There are many ways that reassurance-seeking behaviors play out. In the above example, Natasha relies on asking dating partners about their feelings. Others seeking reassurance may research medical problems online, call doctors, or query friends about a particular problem. The purpose of all these behaviors is the same: to diminish any form of doubt and uncertainty you're struggling with.

Checking

This particular safety behavior is done to make sure you check, verify, or confirm that a particular negative outcome doesn't occur or that a particular thought is not true. Here are some examples:

Jeff, a visual designer, is working on the visual elements for the band Muse's upcoming release. Jeff is passionate about creating aesthetic backgrounds and really strives to do his best to have the perfect colors, images, text, and shapes when creating these visual panels so all those elements can interact organically and shift easily for each song. In his attempt to make sure that everything looks okay, Jeff becomes scared about something *potentially going wrong*. So he checks each element, and when he thinks he's done, he wonders, *What if I made a mistake? What if I didn't focus carefully on the shapes and the coordination of the elements?* As a result, Jeff goes back to check each of the panels, color pixels, sound bites, and every line of coding that was done mixing those elements. What would typically take someone two days of work takes Jeff seven days of looking at all the minutia to make sure that everything is okay.

Checking can also include private experiences. Aleya has an obsession about contracting a respiratory disease, despite doctors telling her that there are no indications in her medical profile. She constantly checks her breathing to see whether she notices a subtle difference in the quality, pace, and temperature of her breathing and how much air is moving through her nostrils, all just to make sure that her breathing is okay.

As you can see, checking behaviors can include both external and internal triggers, and can be external, as in Jeff's case, or internal, as in Aleya's case.

Escape/Avoidance

Think about all the times when you ran, as fast as possible, from an anxiety-triggering situation. Those actions are called *escaping,* and they refer specifically to running away from a situation in the moment. *Avoidance,* in general, includes all the escaping behaviors you do. So escape and avoidance are cousins. When someone runs away from a situation in the moment, psychologists call that escape; when a person develops patterns of behavior to minimize contact with a triggering situation, it's called avoidance.

Let's consider Paco's struggles for a moment. Paco is scared of taking elevators and avoids them at all costs. When he was in high school, he got stuck in one for three hours and had a panic attack; since then he does everything he can to not take one. Paco has been skillfully avoiding elevators by asking others if there are elevators before going to a new place, ensuring that there are stairs, or visiting a building ahead of time to make sure that he can take stairs. Paco has been going out of his way to make sure he never gets trapped in an elevator again. So far, so good. But, as it happens in life, one day he had an interview with a journalist at a coffee shop, and as the conversation unfolded, Paco was invited to go to the editorial department on the seventh floor of the building. Paco felt a rush of fear throughout his whole body, from his toes to his head. He could barely talk. As they got closer to the elevator, Paco's heart was like a drum, and he said, "I'm sorry, I forgot I have another meeting right now. Have to go!" and he quickly walked toward the exit of the building. Paco escaped his anxiety about elevators. But his elevator fear only got worse because avoidance prevented him from learning that he could ride them safely.

Now that you're familiar with how distraction, procrastination, overpreparing, reassurance seeking, checking, and escape/avoidance behaviors can play out in real life, we'll cover the change processes that will help you handle these safety-seeking behaviors as effectively as possible and in a way that helps you break the shackles of anxiety.

Processes That Reduce Safety Seeking

Let's begin. Moving forward with this chapter you will learn two specific skills: response prevention and exposure. Both processes involve developing safety behavior hierarchies, so we'll begin there.

Safety Behavior Hierarchies

Think of all the go-to safety-seeking behaviors you're currently engaging in. These are the ways you cope with situations that, instead of helping you feel less anxious and in control, leave you feeling overwhelmed by uncertainty and every possible calamity that might befall you in life. On the worksheet below, list these safety-seeking behaviors in column two. Next, rate their impact on your day-to-day life, and, last, rank them from most to least impactful (i.e., 1 = most impactful).

Safety-Seeking Behaviors Worksheet

Rank	Habitual Safety-Seeking Behaviors	Impact on Your Day-to-Day Life			
		Minimal	Small to Medium	Large	Huge

Example. When Martha listed and ranked her safety-seeking behaviors, she was surprised to see how many of them had a strong impact on her life and work.

Rank	Habitual Safety-Seeking Behaviors	Impact on Your Day-to-Day Life			
		Minimal	Small to Medium	Large	Huge
11	Avoiding freeways		x		
9	Avoiding crowded places	x	x	x	x
2	Avoiding going out at night	x	x	x	x
6	Checking internet about health concerns			x	
5	Putting off paying bills			x	
1	Putting off tasks at work			x	
10	Avoiding meeting with my boss			x	
7	Seeking reassurance from Bill re: his feelings for me			x	
3	Checking to see if I'm feeling anxious				
4	Checking my heart rate				
14	Seeking reassurance from Margaret (friend) about my dress and appearance				
8	Taking too much time to dress and do makeup—often late for work				
12	Seeking reassurance from Bill that he isn't mad at me				
13	Avoiding people who are sad—Mom				

Every type of safety behavior except escape/avoidance can be reduced or eliminated with a process called *response prevention*—the gradual or complete cessation of the behavior. Escape/avoidance requires a different approach called *exposure*, which you'll learn about later in this chapter.

Response Prevention

Response prevention is what it sounds like: using strategies to prevent you from responding with your typical safety behaviors. You can use response prevention to overcome distraction, procrastination, overpreparing, reassurance seeking, and checking. Start with the safety behavior that's having the greatest impact on your life.

Because safety behaviors in the long run make you more anxious and intolerant of any uncertainty, it's best to stop them altogether. If you can cease a safety behavior cold turkey, that's ideal. But sometimes that's too big a hill to climb because stopping a safety behavior can initially and temporarily raise your anxiety. In this case you can reduce the frequency or onset of your safety behavior. Use the worksheet below to make your safety behavior reduction plan. List the behaviors that have either a large or huge impact on your life, as well as some that have a minimal impact, and their rank. Then, in the third column, write a specific action for each behavior that will help you reduce it (or indicate that it's not needed).

Safety Behavior Reduction Plan

Rank	Habitual Safety-Seeking Behaviors	Reduction/Cessation Plan

Here is how Martha completed her plan:

Rank	Habitual Safety-Seeking Behaviors	Reduction/Cessation Plan
1	Putting off tasks at work	Start working within 24 hrs. of assignment
3	Checking to see if I'm feeling anxious	Set smartphone timer to check every hour, then 3 hrs., then 6 hrs., then once a day, then nothing
4	Checking my heart rate	Same as above
5	Putting off paying bills	Pay on 3rd Saturday of the month
6	Checking internet about health concerns	D/C looking at WebMD
7	Seeking reassurance from Bill re: his feelings for me	D/C asking
8	Overpreparation: dressing/makeup	Set timer for 40 minutes, then go as I am
12	Seeking reassurance from Bill that he isn't mad at me	Not worth working on
14	Seeking reassurance from Margaret about my dress and appearance	Not worth working on

Martha listed the safety behaviors that most affected her life or relationships first. In her case, putting off tasks at work was getting her in serious trouble and creating high levels of anxiety—so she focused on that initially.

Now that you have an inventory of your most important safety-seeking behaviors and a written plan to reduce them, it's time to use response prevention to make changes. When experiencing an urge to distract, procrastinate, overprepare, escape, ask for reassurance, or engage in checking behaviors, follow these steps:

1. **Make a personal commitment** to disengage from relying on your particular safety-seeking behaviors. You can even write it down in a journal or calendar: "I commit to drop [safety-seeking behavior] on [date] so I can be [personal value]." Make sure you are clear why ending your safety behavior will make your life better. What will you be able to do that you can't do now?

2. **Acknowledge that you have an urge** to do safety-seeking behaviors. Pretending it's not there—as you may know by now—will just make things worse. So what about making room for it? You can acknowledge it by simply describing how it feels. You may say to yourself, *I notice this tension in my stomach showing up. I notice this feeling of danger.*

3. **Name your urge.** When you feel a push to do a safety behavior, you can give your urge a name like "The Freak-Out" or "The Pusher." You can choose any name; what's important is that you use that name to recognize the familiar push or urge.

4. **Connect with your body.** Take a deep breath, roll your shoulders back, rotate your head from one side to another. This helps you to be grounded. Observe and release tension. Notice areas of discomfort and breathe into them.

5. **Choose what to pay attention to.** Notice where you're at in the moment, what you are doing, or who you're with. If your mind wanders, refocus your attention on what's important to you right now. What task or work matters at this moment? What relationship is your priority now?

6. **Follow your plan,** allowing any anxious or uncomfortable feelings to rise and gradually recede—just like a wave.

Exposure

Exposure, very basically, involves approaching your fears. Almost everyone has something they fear and avoid, and most people have several. Over the years, most exposure treatments have been based on the *habituation model,* which encourages you to face your fears gradually, in graded steps, and to stay in a triggering situation until your anxiety level decreases. However, despite this model's success, a significant number of people don't respond to it, relapse, and drop out of treatment prematurely (Craske et al. 2014).

Instead of facing fears incrementally and maintaining each exposure until the fear begins to subside, Craske (2013) found that the association between the thing you fear and a sense of danger can be broken by something called *inhibitory learning.* Having multiple experiences of the feared stimulus, in different locations and different ways, creates a "new safe association" that blocks activation of old learning (that the feared stimulus is dangerous) and builds a sense of safety in relationship to the old, feared stimulus. Exposure techniques work best when linked to personal values, so as you learn exposure techniques in the next section, we'll be asking you to revisit the values you identified in chapter 1.

Completing a Values-Based Exposure Worksheet

To start, on the Values-Based Exposure Worksheet that follows, list all the situations you're escaping/avoiding. (You already have them listed in your Safety-Seeking Behaviors Worksheet.) Martha, for example, had five escape/avoidance behaviors on her list:

- Avoiding freeways

- Avoiding crowded places

- Avoiding going out at night

- Avoiding meeting with her boss

- Avoiding people who are sad

She also, on reflection, added two more avoidance experiences:

- Avoiding public transit

- Avoiding people with strong opinions and high standards (like her friend, Marjorie; her coworker, Jim; and her mother—whom she also avoided because she was sad)

Don't worry yet about the columns for your values and ratings. We'll work with those later.

Values-Based Exposure Worksheet

Escape/Avoidance Behavior/ Feared Situations	Value	Value Rating 1–5

Because facing your fears is hard work, it's important that you figure out what you care about—what makes the work worth it—when you approach these scary situations. To clarify your personal values, answer these two questions:

1. Which feared situations matter enough to you that you're willing to face them and sit with the discomfort that comes with approaching them?

2. Which values (things you deeply care about) make it worthwhile for you to do the challenging work of facing those fearful situations?

Then, in column 2, fill in these values for each feared situation. Next, rate each feared situation in terms of how much you value and care about whatever you're avoiding (from 1–5). Each situation is a potential exposure exercise in your Exposure Menu, which we'll work on shortly.

Let's look at Martha's Values-Based Exposure Worksheet:

Escape/Avoidance Behavior/ Feared Situations	Value	Value Rating 1–5
Avoiding freeways	Visit Mom/travel/help in emergencies	4
Avoiding crowded places	Enjoy live music	5
	Civil rights protests	
	Activist meetings	
Avoiding going out at night	Live music	5
	Activist meetings	
	Visiting friends	
	Feeling free/independent	
Avoiding meeting with boss	Working effectively	4
	Keeping my job	
	Collaborative work	
Avoiding people who are sad	Visit Mom	4
	Being supportive to friends in pain	
Avoid public transit	Travel eco-friendly transit	3
Avoid people with strong opinions/high standards	Support my more difficult friends/ colleagues	3

You will use your Values-Based Exposure Worksheet to create your Exposure Menu—a list of multiple exposure activities to decrease your habitual safety-seeking behaviors.

Creating an Exposure Menu

Your Exposure Menu is your road map for tackling those triggering situations in an organized and planned manner. You can always go back to it and adjust it as needed. To create your Exposure Menu, begin with the situations you value most, those you rated in the 3–5 range on the Values-Based Exposure Worksheet. For each situation, think of behaviors and activities you can do to approach the previously avoided situation. If some of those activities are extremely hard, you can add other exposure exercises to make things more doable for you. You don't have to approach a feared situation by immediately jumping in the deep end of the pool. You can always modify. Try considering the following variables:

- Spatial proximity: How close are you going to be to the feared situation?

- Temporal proximity: For how long will you be in contact with the feared situation? (For example, driving on the freeway for 5 minutes, then 10 minutes, then 30)

- Degree of threat: How difficult is the feared situation? Is there a way, at least at first, to make it less threatening? (For example, driving on the freeway in light traffic, then moderate traffic, then at rush hour)

- Degree of support: Is there someone who can be your support person when facing this feared situation? This would help prepare you to eventually face it alone.

Each item on your Exposure Menu can be broken down into multiple exposure opportunities, each one helping to break the association between the old, feared experience and a sense of danger.

Example. Chris, a website developer, is afraid of public speaking and dogs. When he is expected to speak at weekly meetings, his anxiety is prominent: he feels his heart beating fast, sweaty hands, butterflies in his stomach. He wants to be promoted to an executive-level position in his company, but he's extremely concerned about his fear of public speaking, since the new position will require him to run multiple meetings during the week.

Chris has similar anxious reactions when seeing, hearing, or being around dogs. When he was a teenager, he was attacked by a dog, and since then he has been struggling with a dog phobia. He has been successful at avoiding dogs for years by asking his friends to keep their dog in a separate room, not going to parks where dogs could be unleashed, and not leaving his car somewhere until he is sure that no dogs are around. But Chris has fallen in love with someone who's a dog sitter; he knows it's time for him to overcome his phobia.

When Chris answered the two questions from above, he came up with the following values:

Career: Leading and inspiring people to do good work

Romantic relationships: Sharing and participating in my partner's interests; being open to new shared experiences

Personal growth: Being willing to face unpredictability, the unknown, and uncertainty as it comes up in my day-to-day life

Relationships: Being authentic when connecting with others

After gaining a sense of his personal values, Chris came up with this Exposure Menu based on how his day-to-day activities are impacted by his fear of social performance and dog phobia.

Exposure Menu

Making a suggestion at a meeting, so I can practice sitting with the discomfort that comes with not knowing how people see me.

Going to a new neighborhood with my girlfriend without asking if she sees a dog around, so I can practice being open to new situations.

Asking a friend who owns a dog to go on a ten-minute stroll with me with the dog leashed at all times, so I can practice being comfortable near dogs.

Making three brief comments in each meeting, so I can learn to be with the discomfort of being the center of attention. I'll do it toward the beginning/middle of the meeting instead of procrastinating or not doing it at all.

Inviting a coworker to go out for lunch, so I can get better at connecting with others.

Being next to a leashed dog for 5 minutes without asking the owner if the dog is aggressive, so I can participate in my partner's interests.

Smiling and asking a question to a stranger about a product in a grocery store, so I can get better at connecting with others.

Driving to a dog park and staying in the car for 10 minutes while watching the dogs playing, so I can learn to try new experiences.

Inviting people to my place for dinner, so I can learn to have open and honest conversations with others.

Writing a brief update on my department and reading it during a meeting, so I can help inspire people to do good work.

Asking my girlfriend about the challenging moments she has had with dogs as a dog sitter, so I can share in her experiences.

Here are important things to notice about Chris's Exposure Menu.

- There is a mixture of exposure exercises related to both of his fearful situations. If you're dealing with different fearful situations, you don't need to have a separate Exposure Menu for each one of those fears, just a single one, like Chris created.

- Chris's exposure activities are related to his day-to-day life. This is the best starting point for approaching your fears. Exposure exercises are not about counting how many times you face a feared situation and power through. They are about making sure that facing a particular situation, person, activity, or object gets you closer to being the person you want to be and doing the things that matter to you.

- Some of the exposure activities also identify the safety crutch that Chris is trying to discontinue during his exposure. This is important, since the purpose of approaching your fears is to get in contact with, to the best of your ability, the emotional experience that shows up in the moment.

Now, let's dive into the different types of exposure exercises you can do.

Types of Exposure Exercises

Three types of exposure exercises—situational, imaginal, and interoceptive—are covered in this chapter. You will learn in detail about each one of them and how to connect them with your values. You can select the best one when working through your exposure menu.

Situational Exposure. This type of exposure means *physically approaching an activity, situation, person, or object and getting in contact with all the discomfort that comes with it.*

Rose has been avoiding driving on the freeway for years, a phobia she manages by asking others to give her a ride wherever she needs to go: school, her girlfriend's apartment, work, and basketball games. When she cannot find a ride, she plans ahead for the extra time it will take her to use public transportation, or she checks if she can afford an Uber. Her Exposure Menu looks like this:

- Driving for 5 minutes with a person sitting in the passenger's seat

- Driving for 5 minutes alone

- Driving for 10 minutes alone

- Driving to school – night class

- Driving to visit my girlfriend – light, then heavy traffic

- Driving to work with coworker who lives nearby

- Driving to work alone

- Driving to a hiking trail

- Driving to the stadium with friends

- Driving to the foothills to do some oil painting, coming home at rush hour

Imaginal Exposure. Another way to do exposure exercises is by using your imagination based on a script you develop for that purpose. Use imaginal exposure when you are dealing with triggering situations that you cannot approach as a situational exposure: for example, obsessional thoughts about stabbing your loved ones, contracting AIDS, or disturbing sexual behavior; the thought of losing or forgetting something; the fear of thunderstorms or being attacked.

Another good time to use imaginal exposure is when you have tried a values-guided situational exposure first, and you're feeling terribly anxious and fearful about that particular situation. You just can't make yourself do it until you practice with a visualized scene.

Here are the key elements to writing a values-based imaginal exposure script:

1. Write the script in the present tense, as if it's happening right now.

2. Write the script in the first person, using "I" as a pronoun.

3. Use as many details as possible that involve the five senses, describing what you see, hear, feel, sense, and smell.

4. Describe your private experiences when having those images or obsessions (for example, "I feel…," "My body will…," "I'm thinking…"

5. Write down the script, including the worst-case scenario.

6. Do not include reassurance statements (for example, "Everything was okay, I was fine," "They were fine," "This would never happen," "This will end soon").

7. Do not engage in mental rituals (such as counting, praying, or saying special words) or distract yourself.

8. Don't worry about the length of the script; it doesn't matter. It's more important to have a script that has the elements described in points 1 through 6.

Imaginal exposures have two steps:

Step 1. Record your imaginal exposure script on your smartphone or a digital recorder. When recording your script, you may experience some degree of discomfort and urges to stop or neutralize your reactions. Do your best to keep talking until you complete recording your full imaginal exposure script.

Step 2. Listen to your imaginal exposure script. Find a comfortable place to listen to your recording, and then play it for at least 30 minutes a day. If you can, set the replay option on your device; if not, do so manually.

The best way to keep track of imaginal exposures is to note your urge to avoid (from 0 to10) every 5 minutes while listening to your recording (0 = no avoidance urge; 10 = maximum avoidance urge). Use the following graph to monitor your avoidance response throughout an imaginal exposure session. The ideal process is to keep listening to the exposure script until you notice some reduction of the avoidance urge.

Imaginal Exposure Monitoring Graph

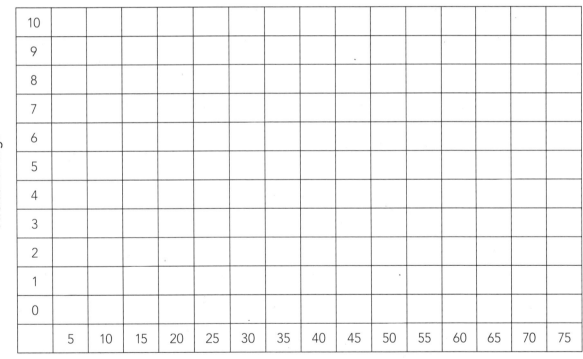

Time (in minutes)

Repeat exposures to the script until the images or thoughts no longer trigger a significant drive for avoidance.

Example. Let's consider Jason, whose sister recently died. He is a very religious person and is experiencing blasphemous obsessions, such as "God doesn't care"; "God is cruel." When having these thoughts, Jason feels guilty and ashamed. He spends hours praying as proof of his faith and as distraction. Jason fears his aloneness and that he will offend or lose his connection to God. His script is an exposure to both fears:

> I'm walking in the street, wandering around and feeling a strong sense of emptiness. It feels like God has left me. He's not protecting me any longer. I'm sad, feeling abandoned, and upset that He's not watching over me. No one is watching over me. I keep walking in the street feeling a strong hollow sensation and pain in my chest. My sense of loneliness is bigger than my existence. I cry quietly while walking in the street; no one notices anything. As I walk, I see so many homeless people, smell bad smells, watch people driving pretentious cars in a rush. Everyone is doing their own thing, nobody cares. Now I have the thought "God doesn't care, God is cruel." I repeat the thought 20 times.

Interoceptive (Physical) Exposure. Sometimes the triggers of a habitual safety-seeking behavior are physical sensations—rapid breathing, feeling hot, feeling tired or heavy, feeling weak or shaky, feeling light-headed or floating, feeling abdominal tension, and many others. Typical safety behaviors for scary physical sensations include distracting, reassurance seeking, checking (to see if they're still there), and escaping/avoiding. But the result of these safety behaviors is more distressing sensations and a constricted life in which you avoid anything you associate with these physical sensations.

For this type of exposure, you need to identify those specific physical sensations that are related to your anxiety episodes. Then do two things:

1. Think about regular physical activities that are part of your day-to-day life that may trigger some of those bodily sensations (for example, if your heart beating fast is a trigger for your fear of having a heart attack or a panic attack).

2. Practice interoceptive exercises that mimic or activate that particular physical sensation.

Here are the most common interoceptive exercises you can start with: holding your breath, breathing very rapidly, swallowing fast, jumping up and down in the same place, breathing through a straw, staring in a mirror, drinking water really fast, running up and down the stairs, staring at a light, smelling strong smells, wearing a scarf around your neck a bit tight, shaking your head from side to another, stretching your muscles for long periods of time so you experience a tingling sensation, or doing abdominal workouts with books on your stomach.

Try each of the above exercises to see which activate distress and avoidance. Then list the ones that do on the Interoceptive Exposure Chart below. These are the interoceptive (physical) experiences that you fear and avoid. Now it's time to actually do exposures with these feared sensations. For each trial, try to stay with the experience at least one minute past the point of anxiety or discomfort. Then rate the experience from 0 to 10 in terms of the urge to avoid. Keep repeating exposures for a given interoceptive experience until the urge to avoid is 3 or below. Then move on to do exposure trials with another feared sensation.

Interoceptive Exposure Chart

Interoceptive Experience	Trial (Rate 1–10)							
	1	2	3	4	5	6	7	8
1								
2								
3								
4								
5								
6								
7								
8								
9								
10								

Recommendations for Your Exposure Exercises

Start your values-guided exposure practice with an activity that truly matters to you, that you're committed to, and for which you're willing to face all the anxiety and discomfort that comes with it. If the exposure exercise gets so challenging that it becomes unbearable, you can always adjust it and make some changes. You can do it for less time, create more distance, or use imaginal exposure first. To maximize your exposures, keep in mind the following principles:

Don't escape by distracting yourself, performing relaxation exercises, doing calming mental rituals, or any other kind of *coping.* It's natural that you may have urges to distract from, escape, or minimize the reaction you have when facing triggering situations—it makes sense. And yet to fully liberate yourself from those fears, worries, anxieties, and obsessions, it's important that you approach those fearful situations exactly as you experience them.

Keep doing your exposure practice as your feelings change. All the feelings of anxiety, fear, discomfort, and distress that come with your exposure practices may go up, go down, or plateau. This is very natural. When practicing exposure exercises, as when doing anything we care about—from cooking our favorite recipe to raising our kids, from applying for our dream job to going on a date— our emotions move in all directions. Don't expect your anxiety always to go down.

Remember your body, mind, and emotions have a life of their own. You can't really control what you feel. But you can choose how to respond to your feelings.

Use acceptance prompts when feeling emotionally overwhelmed. An *acceptance prompt* is a short, gentle reminder that you can accept your anxious feelings and let them go. Watching an overwhelming experience and then letting it go is extremely effective at making painful feelings recede sooner. Here are some sample acceptance prompts:

- *I can allow and make room for this.*

- *I'm willing to have this feeling so I can… (your values-based action).*

- *I want to give my best at this moment to ride this wave of emotion.*

- *I want to do what I can to let this thought or obsession come and go.*

- *Fighting this wave makes it worse.*

- *I'm going to let this one go.*

- *I want to get through this without fighting.*

- *I can accept that I feel (the emotion).*

Be curious when practicing your exposure exercises. Being curious is not a technical principle but a matter of attitude and approach. The attitude of curiosity is one that doesn't get attached to any particular outcome. This curiosity means that, when practicing exposure exercises, you are open to and interested in what shows up, how it shows up, and how often it shows up. Instead of thinking, *I can't have this feeling or sensation,* you observe with interest *everything* you experience.

Following these tips to practice your values-guided exposures—and approaching fearful thoughts, feelings, objects, situations, and people—will help you to maximize the steps you're making, the effort you're putting into it, and the courage you're taking to build the full and meaningful life you deserve!

Processes That Increase Your Inner Safety

While response prevention and exposure exercises can help liberate you from habitual safety-seeking behaviors, the following change processes can help you increase your inner safety.

Observe Your Fear-Based Reactions

Over the next week, devote 15 or 20 minutes a day to observing any fear-based reactions you may have experienced. Here are key principles to follow when observing all the worries, anxieties, obsessions, and fears that may come your way:

Observe. Watch the fear-based reactions as if you're watching them from a little distance.

Label. Give a name to the fear-based reaction you're experiencing.

Don't judge it. Try to accept each fear-based reaction for what it is: one of many emotions you're wired to have and just one of a multitude you'll have over your lifetime.

Don't block or resist it. Don't try to distract yourself, argue yourself out of it, or push these fear-based responses away.

Don't amplify, hold on to, or analyze it. Your task is to watch the fear-based reaction as it comes, not to figure it out, justify it, or explain it.

Practice Uncertainty Workouts

Everyone wants to know the future, to resolve uncertainty by trying to figure out what will happen in any given circumstance. But most of the time life remains uncertain and unpredictable, and it doesn't come with a clear-cut script of what's coming next. So embracing uncertainty and accepting the risk that comes in every choice you make is another skill that you can practice, experience, and grow from.

Here are some exercises for you to practice:

1. Go to a restaurant and try a new dish.

2. Wear a new color that you haven't worn in a while.

3. Interview a person who holds a political view different from yours.

4. Take a cold shower.

5. Change your route to go to work.

6. Try a new haircut.

7. Drink a new flavor of tea.

8. Practice making decisions—small ones—where you have no clear idea of the outcome, but you decide, in advance, to accept whatever happens.

The suggestions above may seem a bit mundane, but here is the reality: trying each one of these activities with a pinch of curiosity, experimentation, and openness to see how it feels, how it sounds, and how it looks will help you to exercise the muscle of living with not knowing. The point is to allow whatever experience shows up, without resisting or predicting what it might be. This is the art of embracing uncertainty.

Summary

In this chapter you learned about six specific safety-seeking behaviors—distraction, procrastination, overpreparing, reassurance seeking, checking, and escape/avoidance and how they impact your day-to-day life. You also learned how to decrease them by using response-prevention exercises, as well as how to find courage to face all the worries, fears, and anxieties that drive them by practicing values-based exposure exercises.

From here, return to the assessment chapter and look at your next highest scores on the Comprehensive Coping Inventory–55. That will tell you which chapter to work on next.

CHAPTER 3

Passion: From Emotion-Driven Behavior to Values-Driven Choices

You have chosen to do the work in this chapter because you scored high on section 3 of the Comprehensive Coping Inventory–55, "Emotion-Driven Behavior." When you feel bad, you tend to automatically act in a way that prolongs the painful feelings and makes them worse. This chapter will help you understand your emotion-driven behavior and learn to react more flexibly when you feel sad, angry, or fearful.

Emotion-Driven Behavior: What It Is

Passionate people feel emotions intensely, whether the feelings are positive, like love and joy, or negative, like anger and sadness. The trouble starts when people put the more negative feelings into action in an automatic, rigid way, in other words, engage in *emotion-driven behavior*. If you're depressed, the emotion drives you to shut down and withdraw repeatedly. In every domain of your life—at home, at school, at work, with friends, with family—you'll tend to be inactive and nonresponsive. You won't participate in what's going on around you, go out, or initiate conversations. It's easy to get trapped in a vicious cycle in which the more you shut down and withdraw, the more depressed you feel.

If you feel angry most of the time, the emotion drives you to behave aggressively. You'll be quick to take offense and short on tolerance. You'll respond to delays, incompetence, or inconvenience with automatic, explosive, hair-trigger aggression. And contrary to the popular misconception that blowing off steam can be helpful, repeatedly expressing your anger only fuels more anger.

If you're anxious, the emotion drives you to avoid certain people, situations, experiences, or things. For example, you may seize any excuse to avoid spending time with your boss or your father-in-law. You may avoid speaking up in a group situation or driving anywhere you haven't been before, or driving at night, on the freeway, or in certain parts of town. Or perhaps you always avoid heights, elevators, or tight, confining spaces. Unfortunately, avoidance only makes your anxiety worse, not better.

If you're plagued by guilt and shame, these emotions drive you into hiding, aggression, or defensiveness. You may try not to be noticed by other people and mainly stick to the margins and shadows of life. If you're caught in the smallest error or inconsistency, you might lash out in anger or become excessively defensive, throwing out a string of explanations and excuses for your mistake. And then you're likely to feel even more guilty and ashamed.

What many people do not realize is that emotion is not a steady state. Emotions come and go in waves that typically pass in about 5 minutes. This means that if you refrain from acting on a painful feeling, if you can wait it out, it will subside and you will feel better in a relatively short time. But if you immediately give in to the urge to act aggressively or avoid a frightening situation, you will often end up prolonging the bad feelings. Emotion-driven behavior prevents you from riding out the wave and makes anger, sadness, shame, and fear worse, prolonging your suffering.

In the long run, emotion-driven behaviors damage your personal and work relationships. For example, when Paula got angry with her brother, her first impulse was to curse him out, listing all his faults and failings, until she had run him out of her apartment. She ended up driving him away permanently, depriving herself of the one relative who had any interest in supporting her.

Emotion-driven behaviors also make it hard to live according to your values. George believed it was important for him to keep his promises, to deal fairly with others, and to support his family. But when George's anxiety about his job performance got intense, he would call in sick, leading to his eventual firing for absenteeism. He felt extreme guilt for failing to live up to his values and letting others down.

Processes That Reduce Emotion-Driven Behavior

The exercises in this section will teach you how to:

- become aware of the waves of your emotions and your "action urges"

- examine the "emotion communicators" underlying your emotion-driven behavior

- create a plan to do the opposite of your emotion-driven behavior

- actually *do* the opposite

- practice behavioral delay

- use visualization to consider what your ideal self would do

Visualize and Observe Your Emotions

In this visualization exercise, you will relive a past emotional upset and observe the components of an emotion, with special attention to the "action urge" associated with the emotions. Pick a situation from your past in which you felt very angry, sad, ashamed, afraid, or anxious. It's a good idea to record the following instructions, pausing after each paragraph so you have time to observe and describe your experience.

Find a quiet place to practice where you won't be disturbed. Sit or lie in a comfortable position with your eyes closed. Take several deep breaths, concentrating on the air entering and exiting your lungs.

Visualize the scene you've chosen in detail and watch the difficult emotion arise. Notice the feeling and keep your attention on it until a word or phrase comes to mind that labels the emotion. Just say to yourself, *Right now I'm feeling* _____. Notice how strong the emotion is and rate it on a scale of 0 to 10.

Rerun the scene in slow motion and notice the wave-like progress of the emotion. Watch as the bad feeling begins with the slightest sense of discomfort and unease, then grows and intensifies like a gathering wave. Notice how the wave of feeling builds to a crest of pain, the point where the anger or fear or sadness peaks and you feel that you have to do something about it.

Pay particular attention to the action urge. When the painful feeling is most intense, what do you want to do? Pinpoint the exact moment of choice, when your distress peaks and you most want to scream, cry, hit something, run away, or hide. How would you put that action urge into words? Tell yourself, *I want to* _____.

Now imagine that you do not perform the action. Imagine that you feel the impulse to act, but you decide not to act upon your feelings. What is it like to feel the urge without acting on it?

If thoughts arise, particularly judgments, just say to yourself, *Now I'm having* _____ (angry, sad, or anxious) *thoughts* or *Now I'm having judgments about* _____ (myself or my emotion). Just label the thought and then let it go.

Repeat this visualization with other scenes from your history of emotion-driven behavior. Each time, focus on the feelings as they arise, crest, and lead to an action urge. Name your emotion and describe what you want to do at the moment of choice.

When Lil did this exercise, she visualized the time her college roommate organized a surprise party for her. She saw herself entering their dorm room, seeing the five or six people crowded in there, and hearing them yell, "Surprise!" She felt her shame and embarrassment kick off at that moment. The feelings of exposure, too much attention, and other people's judgment started spiraling up like flames as she blushed and clamped her hands over her face. She recalled vividly her growing urge to flee, to turn around and run from the room.

Detail Your Emotion-Driven Behavior

In order to change your emotion-driven behavior, you need to examine your *emotion communicators:* the words, gestures, postures, facial expressions, and tones of voice that communicate how you feel. Emotion communicators are what you touch or pick up or put down, how you hold your body, where you look or don't look, what you say or don't say, the words you choose, your tone of voice, and so on.

You may be surprised to learn that words play a relatively small role. Only about 40 percent of your meaning is conveyed by the words you choose. The other 60 percent is conveyed by body language, facial expression, situation, and tone of voice. That's why emails are so frequently misunderstood—they consist entirely of words, without the body language and tone of voice that convey so much of what people communicate.

Emotion communicators work in two directions: outward to your audience, and inward to yourself. In addition to conveying information to others, your body language and tone of voice also tell *you* how you're feeling. In this way, your tone, posture, and gestures create a feedback loop that reinforces depression, anxiety, shame, and other mood states. So when you're sad, saying, "I'm sad" is only part of the story. The rest comes across in your quiet tone of voice, downcast eyes, slumped shoulders, shrugs, and grimaces. And when you feel your own posture and hear your own voice, you think, *Wow, I'm really down. I am so depressed,* and this deepens your depression further.

When someone is angry and acts out, it's not so much the insults and curses that frighten people. It's the yelling, the raised fist, the frowning, the red face, and so on. And all of those nonverbal cues are also telling the angry person, *Jeez, look how pissed off I am. I'm really furious,* which heightens and prolongs the rage.

If being on a high floor in a hotel makes you anxious, you might tell the clerk who offers you a room on the thirty-fifth floor, "I don't think so." The words themselves are pretty neutral. Your nervousness will be conveyed by the tremor in your voice, the widened eyes, the upward glance, how you pull your elbows closer to your sides, and the slight protective hunch of your shoulders. And as these bodily cues feed back to you, you tell yourself, *Look how terrified I am by just the thought of the thirty-fifth floor,* and your fear increases.

Guilt or shame might lead a shopper to blurt out, "I'm sorry" and leave a store before completing a purchase. Again, the words themselves are conventional and almost meaningless in casual conversation. However, the clerk will pick up on the shopper's feelings of shame and inadequacy through the ingratiating smile that doesn't match the frowning eyebrows, the wringing of the hands, the falling or sobbing cadence of the voice, the turning away, and the abrupt departure. These emotion communicators will also tell the shopper, *Oh, no! I'm so ashamed I can't even function like a normal person.*

The Emotion Communicators Worksheet that follows will help you explore the details of what you do in challenging situations that tend to provoke emotion-driven behavior. It breaks down emotional expression into four key components: actions and words (what you say), posture and gestures, facial expressions, and tone of voice. Use the worksheet to analyze, in detail, your emotional expression in three or four situations in which you experience painful feelings. When thinking about which difficult situations to analyze here, choose situations that occur frequently in your life, that result in emotion-driven behavior that has negative consequences for you, and that happen predictably, in circumstances you can plan for. You can download and print a copy of this worksheet from http://www.newharbinger.com/50218 for working with other challenging situations in the future.

Emotion Communicators Worksheet

Situation	Emotion	Actions and Words	Posture and Gestures	Facial Expressions	Tone of Voice

Example. Here is how Casey filled out her worksheet:

Situation	Emotion	Actions and Words	Posture and Gestures	Facial Expressions	Tone of Voice
Son's room is a mess.	Anger	Grab him, shake his shoulders, say, "Look at this mess!"	Tower over him.	Frowning, jaw and mouth tight.	Shouting, sounding mean.
Giving verbal report at meeting.	Fear	Look down at papers, breathe shallowly and rapidly.	Slumped down in chair.	Lowered eyes, apologetic.	Quiet, quivery.
Jack says, "Let's go for a run."	Sad, lethargic, hopeless	Lie, say I can't because I'm too tired or busy.	Shoulders down, shake head, shrug.	Rueful smile, rub closed eyes.	Quiet, tired.
Didn't visit Dad again this week.	Guilt, shame	Avoid thinking about it, keep busy, rush around.	Tense, frenetic.	Frowning, wincing.	Silence (don't talk about Dad or call him).

Plan to Do the Opposite

Now that you've broken down some typical responses into concrete details, this exercise will help you plan the specifics of how you'll do the opposite of these behaviors. Again, you may want to download and print a copy of the worksheet for working with doing the opposite in future situations. In the "Old" column, write the details you included in the Emotion Communicators Worksheet for each situation. In the "New" column, write new and opposite actions and words, posture and gestures, facial expressions, and tone of voice that you plan to put in place.

Plan to Do the Opposite Worksheet

Situation 1:		
	Old	New
Action and words		
Posture and gestures		
Facial expressions		
Tone of voice		

Situation 2:		
	Old	New
Action and words		
Posture and gestures		
Facial expressions		
Tone of voice		

Situation 3:		
	Old	New
Action and words		
Posture and gestures		
Facial expressions		
Tone of voice		

Situation 4:		
	Old	New
Action and words		
Posture and gestures		
Facial expressions		
Tone of voice		

Here is Casey's plan for doing the opposite:

Situation 1: Son's room is a mess.		
	Old	New
Action and words	Grab him, shake his shoulders, say, "Look at this mess!"	Take step back, hands in pockets, and ask, "Do you like it like this?"
Posture and gestures	Tower over him.	Lean against doorway or wall.
Facial expressions	Frowning, jaw and mouth tight.	Smiling.
Tone of voice	Shouting, sounding mean.	Quiet, curious.

Situation 2: Giving verbal report at meeting.		
	Old	New
Action and words	Look down at papers, breathe shallowly and rapidly.	Take a deep breath, look up, and make eye contact.
Posture and gestures	Slumped down in chair.	Sit up straight, lean forward.
Facial expressions	Lowered eyes, apologetic.	Smile.
Tone of voice	Quiet, quivery.	Speak loudly and confidently.

Situation 3: Jack says, "Let's go for a run."		
	Old	New
Action and words	Lie, say I can't because I'm too tired or busy.	Stand up right away and say, "Good idea!"
Posture and gestures	Shoulders down, shake head, shrug.	Shoulders back, nod head.
Facial expressions	Rueful smile, rub closed eyes.	Big smile, eyes wide open.
Tone of voice	Quiet, tired.	Bright and enthusiastic.

Situation 4: Didn't visit Dad again this week		
	Old	New
Action and words	Avoid thinking about it, keep busy, rush around.	Stop what I'm doing, pull out my phone to call and tell him when I'll visit.
Posture and gestures	Tense, frenetic.	Sit down and relax.
Facial expressions	Frowning, wincing.	Smile.
Tone of voice	Silence (don't talk about Dad or call him).	Warm and loving.

Do the Opposite

Now for the hard part: actually doing the opposite. Pick the easiest, least threatening situation to start with, then commit to doing the opposite in a particular situation with a particular person. As the situation unfolds and you feel the familiar anxiety, sadness, or whatever else, remember your plan. Take the actions you outlined above and say what you intend to say, adopt the posture and use the gestures you planned, force your face into the intended expression, and be sure your tone of voice supports doing the opposite. Afterward, evaluate the experience with these questions in mind:

1. How did you do? Be kind to yourself and realize that you won't get it 100 percent right the first time.

2. More importantly, how did you feel? Did your usual feelings decrease or change in any way? Did you experience any emotions that felt new in that situation?

3. What did you learn that will help you do better next time? Incorporate these new ideas into your plan.

Use the last question to improve and fine-tune your plan for the next time you find yourself in that situation. If you struggle with doing the opposite, here are some tips that may help:

• Select an easier person or situation to start with.

• Create reminders so you won't forget to follow through on your commitment.

• Share your plan and your commitment to it with someone who cares about you.

• Do part but not all of what you planned, and then gradually do more.

Work your way through all of the situations you explored above, from least to most difficult. In each case, do the opposite, evaluate your results, and revise your plan for that situation accordingly. Continue until you've done the opposite successfully in all of the problem situations you described above. At that point, you'll have enough practice to begin incorporating this skill into your day-to-day life. You may want to continue to analyze your old responses and draw up plans for doing the opposite, or you may find that this skill starts to come more naturally.

The previous exercises mostly drew upon previous experiences from your life. This section focuses more on the future. Going forward, how will you deal with new stressful situations as they arise? How will you deal with your painful feelings and the actions urges you feel?

Practice Behavioral Delay

Many times the best immediate response to a stressful situation is to pause. Just do nothing for a moment. This takes advantage of the transitory nature of emotion, giving bad feelings time to ebb. It also short-circuits the automatic, reflexive nature of emotion-driven behavior. The instructions are very simple, little more than the folk wisdom that advises angry people to count to ten. At the moment of any strong emotion and action urge:

- Take a mental step back from the situation.

- Observe what's going on, your thoughts, your feelings, and your action urge.

- Name your emotion and action urge.

- Take ten breaths and focus on your breathing rather than on your thoughts and feelings.

- Ask what Buddhists would call your *wise mind*, "What would my ideal self do here?"

- Choose your response—what the wisest, best version of you would do.

Visualize Your Ideal Self

This visualization exercise develops your sense of your ideal self—who you would be and how you would act if you could calm yourself in any emotional storm and act wisely according to your most cherished values. It's a good idea to record the following instructions, pausing after each paragraph so you have time to observe and describe your experience.

Find a quiet place to practice where you won't be disturbed. Sit or lie in a comfortable position with your eyes closed. Take several deep breaths, concentrating on the air entering and exiting your lungs.

Imagine a likely scene you might encounter in the near future, some situation that would tend to make your worst feelings come up to plague you. Spend a couple of minutes detailing the scene, including who's there, what they do and say, and the sights, sounds, smells, and textures. Make it as real as you can.

Unlike the previous visualization in this chapter, do not make any effort to actually feel the emotions of the scene. Remain somewhat detached, observing yourself in the scene rather than trying to reexperience all the feelings.

From this more detached point of view, describe your emotion and action urge, in the third person, like you are watching a movie. For example, you might say, "She's scared, she wants to leave," or "He's really angry, he wants to yell and break something."

Imagine you are watching your ideal self, the version of yourself who is a little older, wiser, and calmer. This version of yourself can wait out the strong feelings. This ideal self can resist the action urges and do the opposite. This version of you can take the longer view and act according to your values, even in stressful situations like this.

Describe in the third person what this ideal self feels, wants to do, and does instead. For example, you might say, "She's scared, she wants to leave, but instead she walks to the front of the class and takes a seat." Or you might say, "He's really angry, he wants to yell and break something. But instead he sits down and asks a question in a quiet voice."

In a few words, describe your ideal self's values, strength, or virtues in this scene, as if describing a hero in a movie or novel. You might say, "She's brave, she's strong, she's determined to learn," or, "He's rational, controlled, and compassionate."

When you are ready, recall your actual circumstances, open your eyes, and go about your day with a clearer vision of your ideal self.

You can repeat this visualization any time you are approaching an emotional situation or other future challenge to how you want to live your life.

Processes That Increase Values-Driven Choices

If you're having trouble putting the above change processes into practice, consider the threefold benefits of changing emotion-driven behavior into values-driven choices. First, pushing through your painful feelings to do the opposite of your usual emotion-driven behaviors will let you in on a valuable secret about difficult feelings: they are neither permanent nor fatal. All feelings come to a peak, subside, and go away, leaving you calmer and more functional on the other side. Second, acting contrary to your feelings will give you a sense of empowerment—a sense that you're more in control. And third, it will allow you to participate more fully in your life, living according to your values rather than your fears and doubts.

Examining Personal Benefits

Let's take a look at one of the change processes you learned: do the opposite. To highlight the personal benefits of doing the opposite, consider each of the situations you worked with in this chapter and make a list of the benefits you hope to gain. You might want to make several copies of the blank worksheet so you can use it for multiple situations, or you can just list the benefits on a separate piece of paper.

Benefits of Doing the Opposite

Relationship with your spouse or partner: _____

_____

Relationship with friends and family: _____

_____

Work or school: _____

_____

Financial: _____

_____

Living situation: _____

_____

More time, energy, or opportunity for: _____

_____

Safety and security: _____

_____

Long-term goals: _____

_____

If you haven't already started working on doing the opposite, now is the time to make a written commitment to do so. Pick the least threatening situation on your list and write down precisely when, where, and with whom you will first do the opposite. Then follow through on your commitment.

When I'll do it: _____

Where I'll do it: _____

With whom I'll do it:_____

Applying Opposite Behavior Across Situations

Changing emotion-driven behavior when you feel anxious is a matter of turning toward and approaching whatever you would normally turn away from and avoid. For example, during the lunch hour at a conference, instead of slipping away to eat a quiet, solitary lunch, you'd accept your coworkers' invitation to go to a restaurant and, once there, you'd actively engage in the conversation.

If you're feeling depressed and would normally throw the day's mail on the dining room table, where it accumulates for weeks, instead do the opposite: open the mail right away, sort it, pay the bills, throw out the junk, and so on. Keep up with the mail daily and keep the dining room table clear of everything but fresh flowers.

For anger, doing the opposite involves changing your usual gestures, tone of voice, and how quickly you respond to provocation. If you'd normally respond to your father's political opinions with sarcastic interruptions, escalating to loud name-calling and pounding on the table, instead listen respectfully until your father finishes a sentence. Then keep your hands in your lap and ask a neutral question in a calm tone of voice; for example, "That's an interesting way of looking at it. How did you arrive at that conclusion?"

If you feel ashamed and guilty, you might enter a family reunion with your head down and shoulders slumped, and then slip into a seat in the corner without making eye contact or saying hello to the others in the room. To do the opposite, walk briskly into the room with your head and shoulders up, stride over to your aunt, greet her enthusiastically, and give her a big hug.

Sustaining Changes Over Time

It will take two to six months to make a habit of doing the opposite of your emotion-driven behaviors. As you practice these powerful techniques, you'll have surprising successes, occasional setbacks, and periods when you seem to plateau and nothing changes for a while. But over time, you will form new habits of reacting to old painful feelings that lessen those feelings and help make them more short-lived.

Eventually, difficult feelings will become a signal to automatically employ opposite action. You'll be able to consistently make values-driven choices. You'll react almost unconsciously, accepting previously overwhelming emotions and allowing them to arise, subside, and flow through you without disrupting your life or controlling your behavior.

Summary

In this chapter you have learned to curtail your emotion-driven behavior and react to challenging situations and feelings with actions that are more in line with your values. This will make it easier to focus passionately on your long-term goals rather than being pushed off course by momentary feelings.

From here, return to the assessment chapter and look at your next highest scores on the Comprehensive Coping Inventory–55. That will tell you which chapter to work on next.

CHAPTER 4

Resilience: From Distress Intolerance to Pain Acceptance

You have turned to this chapter because you scored high on section 4 of the Comprehensive Coping Inventory–55, "Distress Intolerance." You are frequently overwhelmed by your strong feelings.

Many people struggle with overwhelming emotions. Stressful triggering events often lead to strong emotional reactions that leave them feeling besieged and unstable. A major cause of frequent, overwhelming emotions is a vulnerability called *distress intolerance.* Put simply, distress intolerance is the reluctance to face and deal with distressing experiences—things that happened either to you or inside of you, such as painful emotions or sensations.

High scores on distress intolerance indicate the likelihood that this vulnerability is making it hard for you to face painful experiences, resulting in overwhelming emotional reactions. Distressing events lead to intense emotional and physiological reactions, which in turn create emotion-driven behaviors that only make things worse. Increased distress tolerance results in less intense emotional reactions and better control of emotion-driven urges that can wreck your life. This chapter will give you skills to feel more resilient and accepting as you face stressful experiences with the goal of protecting you from feeling emotionally overwhelmed.

Distress Intolerance: What It Is

Distress intolerance is three things: (1) the belief that you can't face or deal with a stressful event or the resulting emotion/sensation; (2) non-acceptance of painful experiences, external or internal, and the insistence (though often not possible) that it stop; and (3) a lack of coping skills to ride the wave of an emotional reaction.

Of course, the opposite is true for distress tolerance: (1) you believe that you possess resiliency to face stressful events, emotions, and sensations; (2) you accept painful experiences when they arise, with a willingness to ride them out; and (3) you have confidence in your skills to cope.

The suite of distress tolerance skills you'll learn in this chapter comes from dialectical behavior therapy, a treatment developed by Marsha Linehan (1993). Multiple studies have provided strong evidence that learning distress tolerance (resiliency) skills reduces the frequency and intensity of disturbing emotions and problematic emotion-driven behaviors (aggression, withdrawal, avoidance). In other words, greater distress tolerance creates greater emotional and behavioral stability.

The processes you will learn to increase acceptance—of both external stresses and your internal emotional and physical reactions (called private events)—were developed by Hayes, Strosahl, and Wilson (1999) as components of acceptance and commitment therapy. Multiple studies have demonstrated their efficacy in reducing emotional distress and increasing behavioral flexibility (freedom from emotion-driven behaviors).

Increasing distress tolerance has three outcomes: (1) You achieve greater resiliency in the face of negative events. (2) You learn to ride resulting waves of sadness, fear, or anger without becoming overwhelmed or destabilized. (3) You greatly reduce aggression, avoidance, and withdrawal behaviors that damage relationships and make life more painful. You then gain a sense of confidence in your ability to choose more effective responses to emotional surges in place of emotion-driven behaviors.

Processes That Reduce Distress Intolerance

In this section you'll learn several strategies for reducing distress intolerance. Once you find the ones that work best for you, you'll find that they are a tremendous help in managing both daily distress as well as more occasional challenging situations.

Letting Go Technique

Distress tolerance starts with learning how to interrupt painful emotional reactions. The letting go technique is a very effective strategy, derived from a method called eye movement desensitization and reprocessing (EMDR). The technique involves *bilateral stimulation* (moving your eyes from one side to the other, tapping one knee and then the other, or tapping one shoulder and then the other), which has the effect of disrupting neuropathways that carry negative thoughts and emotions. It results in a diminished awareness of the feelings and thoughts that pound you when you're distressed. The procedure is simple:

- Whenever you feel emotionally distressed, notice any upsetting thoughts that are present. Observe whatever feelings accompany those thoughts. Now do a round of bilateral stimulation. For example, move your eyes back and forth between corners of the room or tap one knee or shoulder and then the other. Do it twenty-five times.

- As you finish the eye movement or tapping, notice your distress level. If it's still significantly high, repeat the procedure. This "letting go technique" is dose related—the more you do it, the more you feel relief from upsetting thoughts and feelings.

- Whenever a painful thought or feeling threatens your emotional stability, repeat this process. Do the eye movement or tapping twenty-five times. Remind yourself that the pain is temporary and you have the skills and resources to ride it out.

- Wait. Emotions average 1–7 minutes in length. It's a wave you can ride until the attacking thoughts and painful feelings begin to diminish. Take a breath, do your bilateral stimulation, and wait for the slow dawning of relief.

Diaphragmatic Breathing

When you're upset, your breathing becomes fast and shallow. By consciously slowing your breathing and taking air deep into your belly, you send your body the message that everything is all right and there's no need to panic or be upset. Diaphragmatic breathing is simple, but its stress-relieving effects are dramatic. The diaphragm is a wide, strong sheet of muscle beneath the lungs. When you inhale, your diaphragm moves down, pushing your stomach and drawing air into your lungs. When you exhale, the diaphragm moves up to push air out of your lungs. Here are detailed instructions on how to practice diaphragmatic breathing.

Find a quiet place where you won't be disturbed for 5 minutes. Sit up straight and put one hand on your stomach. Close your eyes and take a slow, deep breath in through your nose. Feel how your stomach pushes out against your hand. Then exhale slowly through your mouth, noticing how your hand moves inward again. Continue to breathe in and out slowly and deeply, feeling your hand moving out and in with each breath.

Notice how each inhalation expands your stomach like a balloon. Also notice how your body feels more and more relaxed as you continue to breathe this way. Try to keep your focus on your breath. If your mind wanders, you can try counting during each breath to focus your attention on your breathing. Slowly count to 4 as you inhale, then slowly count to 4 again as you exhale.

Practice diaphragmatic breathing for 5 minutes twice a day, or whenever you feel the need to relax.

Body Awareness

The relaxing effect of this exercise relies on the fact that you can't feel tense and nervous when all your muscles are in a state of relaxation.

Find a quiet spot where you can lie down and not be disturbed. Lie on your back with your legs uncrossed and your hands at your sides. Close your eyes. Take a long, slow breath, and put your attention on your feet. Become aware of any tension you're feeling in your feet. Say to yourself, *Calm, Relax, Serene, Easy,* or another cue word of your choice. As you say the cue word, imagine any tension draining out of your feet.

Next, move your attention up to your calves and shins. Notice any tension in your lower legs, and say your cue word to yourself. As you say the word to yourself, imagine any tension draining out of your calves and shins.

Next, do the same thing with your upper legs—the large muscles in your thighs. Continue moving your relaxing attention up your body: to your buttocks, then your stomach, then your chest, then your back, and then your shoulders. For each area of the body, become aware of any tension, then say your cue word and let the tension fade away.

Next, do the same for your hands, then your forearms, then your upper arms, then your neck, and finally your head, in each case noticing any tension and using your cue word to dissolve the tension. When you've scanned your entire body in this way, you will have significantly reduced your overall muscular tension, profoundly relaxing your body.

Practicing this exercise once or twice a day for a week will teach you a lot about where you carry tension in your body. It will also make you much more adept at relaxation.

Cue-Controlled Relaxation

Once you've gained some experience and skill with the body awareness exercise, you can use your cue word for quick relaxation anywhere, any time.

Inhale. Close your eyes for just a few seconds and scan your entire body for tension. Notice where your muscles are tight, and say to yourself, *Relax, Calm,* or whatever cue word you like, and let your whole body relax as you exhale. Repeat five times, noticing the release you feel in your muscles and the growing sense of relaxation. Allow your whole body to relax with each breath.

Use cue-controlled relaxation in any moment of stress where you fear losing control and need immediate relief.

Safe Place Visualization

This exercise takes advantage of the fact that your mind and body will react to an imaginary peaceful scene almost as strongly as they would to a real location. Think of a place, real or imagined, that makes you feel safe and happy. It can be someplace from your childhood, a vacation spot, a church or temple, a setting from a book or movie, or even a historical setting—absolutely anywhere you like. If you can remember the following instructions, just close your eyes and paraphrase them to yourself. Otherwise, you might want to record the instructions in a calm, quiet voice, and play them back until you've practiced this technique a few times and are familiar with the process.

Find a quiet place where you won't be disturbed for 20 minutes. Sit in a comfortable chair with your feet flat on the floor and your arms relaxed in your lap or on the arms of the chair. Close your eyes and take a deep breath, inhaling through your nose. Hold your breath for 5 seconds, and then exhale slowly. Take another deep breath, hold it for 5 seconds, and once again release it slowly. Continue to breathe slowly and deeply without counting or holding your breath.

Imagine that you're entering your safe place. Use your sense of sight first, and imagine seeing the shapes and colors of the place. Fill in the details. Are there any people or animals there? Watch them do whatever they're doing. If your safe place is inside, notice what the walls and furniture look like. If it's outside, observe the sky, the horizon, the ground, and any plants or water. Continue to observe until you have a clear, vivid, visual impression of your safe place.

Next, concentrate on your sense of hearing. Can you hear the wind? Waves? People talking? Is there music? Do you hear any birds or animals? Choose something soothing to hear.

Next, notice what there is to smell in your safe place. Perhaps it's a scent you remember fondly from your childhood, like flowers or freshly baked bread. If you're outside, smell the ocean, the grass, or whatever aromas surround you. Take a moment to enjoy the fragrances.

Next, notice what you can feel with the sense of touch. Are you sitting or standing in your safe place? Is there any breeze against your skin? Is it warm or cool? Focus for a moment on what your sense of touch can tell you about this place.

Continue to enjoy your safe place, breathing slowly and evenly and noticing what you see, hear, smell, or feel. Realize how safe, relaxed, and content you are. This is your personal, private safe place, and you can return to it at any time. Whenever you feel sad, afraid, angry, or guilty, you can come here for a break and feel the same sense of relaxation and security.

Look around one more time and fix the details in your mind. Now focus again on your breathing. When you feel ready, open your eyes and return your focus to your surroundings.

You can practice this exercise whenever you need a soothing mini-vacation. Once your safe place has become very familiar to you, you can close your eyes for a few seconds during any busy day, visualize your safe place briefly, and feel calmer and more relaxed.

Self-Soothing Techniques

Below, you'll find soothing activities organized by the five senses: touch, sight, smell, taste, and hearing. All are designed to give you a soothing moment of peace. But people are different in what they find most soothing. Look over the lists and choose activities that are likely to soothe you, and also be willing to try new activities to see how they work. Some people find jazz or classical music very relaxing, while others find it energizing or agitating. If you try a suggested activity and it doesn't feel soothing or actually makes you feel worse, move on to another activity.

Self-soothing with touch. The skin is the body's largest organ. It's loaded with sensitive nerves, and no matter what the circumstances, you're always touching something. People differ in their tactile preferences. Check off any of the items below that you're willing to try.

- ☐ Carry a soft, velvety piece of cloth, a smooth polished stone, or worry beads in your purse or locker to touch when you need to.

- ☐ Take a hot or cool shower and enjoy the feeling of the water falling on your skin.

- ☐ Take a bubble bath or a bath with scented oil.

- ☐ Massage your own sore muscles.

- ☐ Play with your pet.

- ☐ Wear clothes that feel good against your skin.

Self-soothing with sight. A very large portion of the human brain is dedicated to visual processing, making sight the most important sense for gathering information about the world. Any given visual stimulus can be very soothing or very alarming, depending on your personal associations. Check off any items below that you're willing to try, and consider adding some of your own visual experiences:

- ☐ Make a collage using pictures you like from magazines.

- ☐ Carry soothing pictures with you in your purse or wallet or on your phone to look at any time you want.

- ☐ Visit some of your favorite places. Go to a park or museum and just sit and look.

- ☐ Hang art on your walls. Put up a painting or photo that you find beautiful or soothing.

- ☐ Look at picture books. Go to a bookstore or a library and find a collection of nature photos or paintings that you love looking at.

- ☐ Draw or paint images that are soothing to you.

- ☐ Carry a photo of someone you love, admire, or just like looking at.

Self-soothing with smell. The sense of smell is very powerful in its ability to bring up memories and evoke certain feelings, so it's important to find aromas that make you feel calm and relaxed. Check any items below that you're willing to try, and add some ideas of your own as well:

- ☐ Burn scented candles or incense.

- ☐ Wear cologne, perfume, or a scented oil that makes you feel confident, happy, or relaxed.

- ☐ Visit places that feature your favorite aromas, such as a bakery, restaurant, or florist.

- ☐ Bake chocolate chip cookies or make other foods that smell particularly good to you.

- ☐ Enjoy outdoor smells. Go out in your yard or to the park and enjoy smells of earth, flowers, and freshly mowed grass.

- ☐ Buy flowers for your home or take a walk and seek out favorites in your neighborhood.

- ☐ Hug someone whose scent makes you feel good.

Self-soothing with taste. Taste is also a powerful sense for awakening memories and feelings, and eating foods you love can be very soothing. However, eating may be a problem for you if you tend to eat too much, binge, purge, or habitually restrict your diet. In that case, use other senses for self-soothing. If eating isn't a problem for you, check off the activities below that you'll try, and add some ideas of your own:

- ☐ Enjoy your favorite food, dish, or meal, eating slowly and savoring every bite.

- ☐ Carry favorite foods with you to snack on when you're upset.

- ☐ Have an occasional treat, like ice cream, pudding, or candy.

- ☐ Drink your favorite beverage, such as coffee, chocolate, or tea. Drink it very slowly, and don't do anything else while you're drinking, so you can really taste the beverage.

- ☐ Suck on an ice cube or ice pop and enjoy the cold, melting sensation.

- ☐ Eat a ripe, juicy piece of fruit very slowly, delighting in its sweet sensations.

Self-soothing with hearing. Certain sounds can soothe and relax you. It could be the sound of a brook, the surf, wind in the trees, bird calls, crickets, or your favorite music. Here are some ideas for soothing yourself with sound:

☐ Create a library of soothing music, accessible on your smartphone. Listen to pieces when you're upset.

☐ Listen to audio books or interesting podcasts.

☐ Listen to peaceful sounds outside your window.

☐ Create a file of soothing nature or water sounds.

☐ Listen to the gentle whoosh of a white noise machine.

☐ Turn on your personal water fountain.

☐ Listen to a recorded meditation.

Distraction

As emotional distress surges, distraction is a proven strategy to get relief by paying attention to something other than your pain. You can distract yourself by…

Paying attention to someone else. When emotions threaten to overwhelm you, bring your awareness to the ones you love. Do something for them. Connect with friends or family to see how they are or who needs help.

Take your attention off yourself by going to a public place. Watch the people there. Observe what they do, focus on the details of their attire and movements. Notice facial expressions, and the emotions you see there.

Redirecting your thoughts. You shift your focus from painful to pleasant thoughts in any of the following ways:

• Remember pleasant events from your past; notice all the details of those happy memories.

• Imagine beautiful places you've been—the sound of the surf on the seashore; meadows surrounded by high mountain peaks.

• Daydream about places you'd like to go or things you'd like to do. Use your imagination to vividly construct these scenes.

• Notice the natural world around you—flowers, trees, landscape, and sky. Listen to the sounds of the wind, of insects, of birds.

- Imagine your wildest fantasy coming true. Who would be there; how would it all unfold?

- Imagine doing something heroic or being praised for a big success.

Leaving. A powerful distraction is to stop what you're doing and change locations. Take a walk and notice the light and shadow, the feeling of the air, the sights and sounds around you. Go onto your deck or into your garden; take a drive to a place that feels relaxing and beautiful.

Doing tasks. Distressing thoughts and feelings can often be eased by focusing on some necessary chore or task. Wash the dishes, do laundry, clean an area of your house, decorate, pay bills, water your plants, do some gardening, get a haircut, cook something tasty and nutritious, and so on.

Counting. Counting is a great method to take your focus off pain. Start with your breath. Count each out-breath till you reach 10 and then start over. Keep counting in groups of 10 till your mind has quieted down and you feel less distressed.

You can also count things you see—the numbers of red cars or Hondas that pass by; the number of trees on each block, the number of houses with a porch, the number of people in white shirts or blouses, the number of brown objects in your office or living room.

Being in the present moment. When your mind is aflame with painful thoughts, you can take refuge in the present moment. Notice everything you see, whatever you hear. Observe how your body comes in contact with the world and how that feels. Are there things right now that you can smell or taste? What is it like inside your body?

By focusing on the sensations of the present moment, you can distract yourself from attacking thoughts and surging emotions. If you are driving, notice the sounds of the tires, the motor; notice the wind coming through the window or the air conditioner; notice the sways and bumps. If you are in a room, notice the temperature of the air, what you're touching, the shapes and colors of the objects around you, the sounds both inside and outside. If you're drinking or eating, notice sensations of temperature and flavor, the experience of lifting your fork or cup, the aromas.

Coping Thoughts

The times when you feel distress are exactly the times you need to hear encouraging words. But you don't often hear them. Coping thoughts are ways you can encourage yourself. They remind you of your strengths and how you survived distressing experiences in the past, and they offer instructions for how to navigate a difficult moment right now. The following coping thoughts are examples of how real people have soothed themselves in the face of emotional pain. They can help you tolerate distressing situations by offering the strength and motivation to endure a painful time. Put a check mark next to the five best coping thoughts that might work for you. Then write them down on an index card or in a notebook that you can refer to in any moment of distress.

- ☐ "This situation won't last forever."

- ☐ "I've already been through many other painful experiences and I've survived."

- ☐ "This, too, shall pass."

- ☐ "My feelings make me uncomfortable right now, but I can accept them."

- ☐ "I can be anxious and still deal with the situation."

- ☐ "I'm strong enough to handle what's happening to me right now."

- ☐ "This is an opportunity for me to learn how to cope with my fears."

- ☐ "I can ride this out and not let it get to me."

- ☐ "I can take all the time I need right now to let go and relax."

- ☐ "I've survived other situations like this before, and I'll survive this one too."

- ☐ "My anxiety/fear/sadness won't kill me; it just doesn't feel good right now."

- ☐ "These are just my feelings, and eventually they'll change."

- ☐ "It's OK to feel sad/anxious/afraid sometimes."

- ☐ "My thoughts don't control my life; I do."

- ☐ "I can think different thoughts if I want to."

- ☐ "I'm not in danger right now."

- ☐ "So what?"

- ☐ "This situation sucks, but it's only temporary."

- ☐ "I'm strong and I can deal with this."

From McKay, Davis, and Fanning (2021).

On the following worksheet, in the column labeled "Distressing Situation," write down up to ten events that can trigger upsetting emotions. In the "Coping Thoughts" column, write down coping thoughts you might use to face and get through these triggering situations.

Coping Thoughts Worksheet

Distressing Situation	New Coping Thought

Example. Here is how Juan completed his Coping Thoughts Worksheet.

Distressing Situation	New Coping Thought
1. Partner complains about me.	1. Let me listen and understand. We've found solutions before.
2. I felt sad – hard to finish a work task.	3. I'll ride this out and not let it get to me.
4. Feeling overwhelmed by missing my father.	5. I'll ride this out; it passes.
6. Anxious at the amount I face – at home and at work.	7. I can be anxious and still deal with the situation.
8. Wrist hurts – flare up of carpal tunnel syndrome.	9. I've dealt with this before, I can overcome it again.
10. Nighttime – sense of loss and aloneness.	11. These feelings are uncomfortable; they'll pass.
12. Sad in the morning – sense of hopelessness.	13. These feelings are uncomfortable; they'll pass.
14. Ticking sound in car motor.	15. I can be anxious and still deal with the situation.
16. Have to travel to Milwaukee.	17. I've taken many trips. These are just feelings; I always get through.
18. Alone at home with my thoughts.	19. My thoughts don't control my life; I do.

Radical Acceptance

A major source of distress is resisting and fighting against painful things that have already happened. Getting angry and upset, blaming yourself or someone else for what happened, telling yourself or others, "It should never have happened," only compounds your pain. Now you have two forms of distress: sadness and regret about a painful event, plus anger or self-blame roiling you on top of it. Insisting that a painful event should never have happened, that it was wrong, a product of bad intentions, is an attempt to undo it. But failure to accept what has happened only makes your distress worse. You're hurt or sad—and in a rage.

You can't change what happened. With *radical acceptance* you can acknowledge what has occurred without judging yourself or others. The chain of events that led to a particular outcome *had to happen*—it was the result of many choices, actions, or circumstances that all eventuated in something hard.

Radical acceptance isn't condoning or agreeing with what happened; it just means you've stopped trying to change something frozen in the past. Here are some suggested coping thoughts to help you face and accept difficult events.

- "This is the way it has to be."

- "All the events have led up to now."

- "I can't change what's already happened."

- "It's no use fighting the past."

- "Fighting the past only blinds me to my present."

- "The present is the only moment I have control over."

- "It's a waste of time to fight what's already occurred."

- "The present moment is perfect, even if I don't like what's happening."

- "This moment is exactly as it should be, given what's happened before it."

- "This moment is a result of a million other decisions."

From McKay, Wood, and Brantley (2019).

Practicing Your Distress Tolerance Skills

On the following worksheet, put a check mark next to the skills from this chapter you'd like to use and master when you're feeling distressed.

DTS (Distress Tolerance Skills)

☐   Letting Go Technique (Bilateral Stimulation)

☐   Diaphragmatic Breathing

☐   Body Awareness

☐   Cue-Controlled Relaxation

☐   Safe Place Visualization

☐   Self-Soothing Techniques

☐   Distraction

   Type:

   _____

   _____

   _____

☐   Coping Thoughts

   _____

   _____

   _____

☐   Radical Acceptance

You can learn and strengthen the skills you checked through a process called coping skills training (Meichenbaum 1977). It starts with visualizing a recent upsetting event, as follows:

Watch the event unfold in your mind. Try to see it like a video, noticing what you and others do and say. Visualize the scene until you feel a moderately strong emotion—around 5 on a 0–10 scale of upset.

Now shut the scene off—stop the visualization—and turn your attention to the emotion itself. For a minute or so, observe the feeling and where it centers in your body. There might be thoughts associated with the feeling. But keep your attention on the emotion itself. In your mind, describe the feeling: its size or intensity; the quality of the emotion.

Now use one of the distress tolerance skills (DTSs) you've decided to learn. Keep using the skill for 1–2 minutes. Now check how distressed you are on the 10-point scale we used earlier. Keep using the coping skill until your distress is down to a 2 or 3 on the scale. If your DTS is working, but slowly, keep coping a little longer until your distress has reduced noticeably.

Repeat the process with a second visualized event.

We recommend that you work on coping skills training once a day, testing and practicing the DTS you selected to learn. Some of the skills you selected may not work well to reduce actual upsetting emotions. Discard them; cross them off the list. Others, with a little practice, will work reasonably well and quickly for upsetting visualized scenarios. These are the DTSs you want to start practicing with real-life events. Using DTSs *in vivo,* at the moment of surging distress, is the goal of coping skills training.

To graduate from practicing with visualized triggers to real-life events, select a DTS you want to utilize and practice each morning. Commit to using it any time you encounter a distressing trigger throughout the day. Commit to practicing a new DTS the following morning. In a week or two, you will have a small, reliable repertoire of DTSs (and will have discarded a few others that don't work so well in real life). Keep a clear intention to practice one or more of your DTSs every time you experience emotional distress.

Example. Sophie had struggled with overwhelming emotions since she was in high school and faced multiple rejections. The distress tolerance skills she felt most interested in learning were:

- Letting Go Technique

- Cue-Controlled Relaxation

- Self-Soothing Techniques: music and beautiful images on her iPhone

- Distraction: redirecting her thoughts by thinking about others, future plans, and positive fantasies

- Coping Thoughts: "I can ride this feeling out. I've done it before, I can do it now. This will pass."

Sophie identified a number of situations where her emotions got the best of her. These included (1) criticism from her partner, coworkers, or friends; (2) sensations of anxiety in the face of work demands; and (3) feeling terrified of abandonment when her partner shrugged and pulled back.

Sophie decided to practice and evaluate her selected DTSs using coping skills training. She visualized details of the triggering situations, allowing the distressing emotions and physical sensations to rise to a mid-level of upset. Then she shut off the image, used her coping strategies, and watched what happened. Some strategies were a bust, and some were really effective, reducing her distress from 5–6 to 1–2. The ones that worked best were:

- Letting Go Technique

- Distracting through future plans

- Cue-Controlled Relaxation with music

- Coping Thoughts

Sophie began practicing the four coping strategies in real life—particularly when she felt criticized (hurt) or anxious. As soon as she noticed the target emotion, Sophie used one or more of her chosen DTSs, keeping at it until the distress was down to 3, or at most 4.

Practicing, and being effective with DTSs, gave Sophie confidence that she could face and ride out upsetting emotions and feelings in her body. She feared her emotions less because she knew she could cope.

A Process That Increases Pain Acceptance

Learning to reduce distress intolerance leads the way to an acceptance of painful emotions, thoughts, and feelings in your body. Instead of resisting or trying to control the pain, you can learn to soften to it, hold it, and simply let the pain be. This new relationship to distress changes painful inner experiences from something bad, something you have to fight, to something you can hold and allow until they morph into another, different experience.

The most effective process for cultivating this change in how you respond to inner pain is the Acceptance Meditation. Rather than attempting to rid yourself of distress, you will learn to allow its presence, let it be without judgment, and watch as the pain changes and eventually subsides.

Acceptance Meditation

Practice the Acceptance Meditation as soon as possible after noticing a distressing feeling or emotion. Take time for this meditation, which takes about 15 minutes, at least once a day. Record the instructions on your smartphone so you can listen to it during your practice.

Begin by getting into a comfortable sitting position. Close your eyes and focus on your breath. Bring your attention to your diaphragm, the center of your breath and life force. Notice each in-breath and mark it by saying, "In." Notice each out-breath and mark it by saying to yourself, "Out." Just keep watching your breath, saying "In" and "Out." (*Pause here*)

As you focus on your breath, thoughts will arise—memories, worries, plans for the future, judgments. Just notice the thought and, as soon as you can, return to your breath. (*Pause here*) Just watch the breath, letting it rise and fall gently and effortlessly. A slow, natural rhythm. (*Pause 2 minutes*)

At this moment, let your attention expand beyond your breath. Let yourself notice where the stress or difficult emotion manifests in your body. You might notice tension, pain, an itch, or just a strange sensation in your body. Just notice it without judging it, and place your attention there for a minute. (*Pause here*)

Next, *soften* toward that stress or difficult emotion in your body. Allow the muscles to release around it. Just notice the feeling or emotion without trying to control or push it away. Your body can be soft around the edges of the feeling, making room for it. Letting go…letting go…letting go of tension around the edges of the feeling. (*Pause here*)

As you're observing, if you experience too much discomfort from an emotion, just do your best to note your experience and return to the rising and falling of your breath; use your breath as your anchor. Do your best not to judge your emotion and not to get distracted by it. (*Pause here*)

Similarly, if a difficult thought arises, do your best to just notice it and let it go. Again, return to the rising and falling of your breath as your anchor. Do your best not to judge yourself or the thought. (*Pause here*)

Now hold the feeling or emotion kindly. Move your hand to cover and hold the spot. Breathe into that feeling. Breathe in a kind regard for that stress or difficult emotion. Think of this place as yours to take care of, to hold as if it were precious and needing your love. (*Pause here*)

Again, if a difficult thought arises, or your mind wanders, notice and accept it. Then let it go. (*Pause here*)

Finally, let this feeling or emotion be. Let it be there without resistance. Let it go or stay. Let it change or not change. Let it be where it is or move. Let it be what it is, making room for it, holding it, accepting its presence in your body and your life. (*Pause here*)

Soften…hold…let be. Soften…hold…let be. Soften…hold…let be. Repeat these words to yourself, holding any pain you may have kindly. Allowing it to stay or leave or change. (*Pause here*)

As you continue, allow difficult thoughts to arise—just noticing them and letting them go. (*Pause here*)

As you continue, you may find that the emotion moves in your body, or even changes into another emotion. Try staying with your experience, continuing to use the mantra of soften-hold-let be. (*Pause here*)

Finally, return your attention to your breath, simply noticing the rising and falling of your breath: breathe in and breathe out. Then, when you are ready, slowly open your eyes when you're finished. (*Close the meditation*)

The Acceptance Meditation here is inspired by Neff and Germer's (2018) "Soften, Sooth, Allow" Meditation and comes from McKay and Wood (2019).

Keep practicing the Acceptance Meditation daily. Its transformative effect takes time, but you will notice over a period of six to twelve weeks that emotions and feelings disturb you less. They're just part of the ever-changing present. You hold them and merely wait. The pain, always and eventually, becomes something else—some new experience—that you can welcome and hold until the next new thing shows up.

Summary

Resilience is something you build rather than find. It is a muscle that strengthens and allows you to ride waves of distress without sinking. In this chapter you have been building resilience in two ways. First, by building coping skills that give you the confidence to face pain and the capacity to turn the knob down on distressing emotions. Second, by increasing acceptance so pain is no longer something you resist or run from. Instead, it becomes something you allow, knowing each moment is different from the last. Resilience is the knowledge that you can face this painful moment and feel it as a bridge to all that follows in your life.

From here, return to the assessment chapter and look at your next highest scores on the Comprehensive Coping Inventory–55. That will tell you which chapter to work on next.

CHAPTER 5

Openness: From Emotion Avoidance to Emotion Acceptance

You have chosen to work on chapter 5 because you scored high on section six of the Comprehensive Coping Inventory–55, "Emotion Avoidance." Emotion avoidance and overcontrol are strategies for coping with sadness, shame, anger, fear, and other strong emotions by masking, hiding, suppressing, or denying the emotional experience altogether (Foa et al. 2019; Hayes and Smith 2005). This might look like distracting yourself, controlling your face to prevent the expression of emotion, faking another emotion, denying emotions to others, spacing out, or even "checking out" entirely, known as dissociating.

The most serious negative outcome of avoiding and suppressing your emotions is that painful emotions become more intense (Linehan 1993; McKay and West 2016). The more you try to avoid anxiety and anxiety-provoking situations, the more anxiety bothers you. The more you avoid sadness, feelings of failure, or grief, the more prolonged and intense these feelings become. Shame only intensifies when you try to block or push it away. And anger becomes a bleeding sore when you refuse to face the pain that drives it. All and all, emotion avoidance only makes emotions bigger and longer lasting.

This chapter will help you cultivate an acceptance of and openness to your emotional experiences, approach very intense feelings with interest and care, and even learn to appreciate what you might think of as "negative" or "bad" emotions. Acceptance makes emotions less overwhelming. You will have more freedom in how you respond to your feelings, choosing when to explore their textures and flavors, and appreciating what you can learn from them, instead of being afraid of their power.

Emotion Avoidance: What It Is

To illustrate emotion avoidance and its repercussions, we'll introduce you to Carmen.

Carmen just had a very difficult conversation with her partner, Tania, who gave her some upsetting feedback. Tania requested that Carmen do a better job staying on top of bills and do her fair share of the chores. Carmen immediately felt a surge of discomfort, embarrassment, anger, and even fear. Her heart rate jumped up right away, she flushed, and her mind immediately started churning out thoughts like *Is she so mad at me that our relationship is in trouble?* and *I'm just a screw-up* and *How dare she say that, she's the one who…* and these thoughts further upset Carmen.

In the face of this strong emotion, Carmen looked away, froze up, and said, "Okay, you're right" to end the conversation. She then retreated to watch Netflix to distract herself for the rest of the evening, talking only very briefly with Tania. The whole next day she experienced surges of that emotion when she thought about the conversation. She tried to get rid of each surge by throwing herself into work, by continuing to binge-watch TV and avoid Tania, and eventually by pouring a glass of wine to "relax."

These responses to strong emotion are understandable, but when Carmen uses emotion avoidance too frequently and too rigidly, it starts to get in the way of her values. In this example, it might prevent Carmen from acknowledging that she wants to be a good partner and that hearing criticism makes her feel vulnerable and afraid for the relationship. Avoiding the emotion might mean avoiding the conversation, or further avoiding the tasks that Tania requested, which might injure the relationship more. The ironic part is that the embarrassment and fear are probably that strong *because* Carmen cares about the relationship—but avoiding those feelings leads to behaviors that make it seem like she doesn't.

Avoiding intense emotions can sometimes be very adaptive, and everyone needs to be able to titrate emotions to some degree. There are certain situations when It's not helpful or even safe to fully feel and express all your emotions—for example, a child growing up in a home where crying is punished, or an adult feeling the pressures of a work environment where talking about your emotions is not accepted. But there are many situations in which It's vital to allow yourself to feel your emotions, explore them for yourself, and express them to others. If avoidance and overcontrol are your go-to ways of reacting to strong emotion, you might get stuck in the habit, or even come to fear or feel shame about your human emotions. This might make it a struggle to feel and communicate when It's vital to do so, and leaves you cut off from the full richness of your feelings. It might also trick you into thinking that you deserve to have your emotions ignored, when really every human deserves care and validation for their feelings!

Emotion avoidance has been linked to a host of issues with self-regulation (De Castella et al. 2018; Gross 1998), can reinforce anxiety-driven avoidance behaviors (Seif and Winston 2014, 109), and can keep individuals trapped in depressive symptoms or inactivity (Persons et al. 2001). Emotion avoidance can cause difficulties with awareness of feelings; ability to label feelings in an appropriate way; and expression of feelings, both verbal and nonverbal (Blaustein and Kinniburgh 2017). There is a lot of evidence to suggest that improving these skills can lead to a reduction in self-reported symptoms of mental illness—including severe anxiety, depression, and emotion dysregulation (Berenbaum et al. 2003). Indeed, even the belief that emotions are dangerous or shameful and must be controlled has been associated with poor outcomes in depression, anxiety, and other clinical problems (Sydenham, Beardwood, and Rimes 2017).

Oftentimes, when emotion avoidance has been your go-to tool in the past, you may not even recognize when you're doing it. So it can help to understand a bit more about emotions themselves.

Emotions are messages sent by the brain to help respond to perceived threats and opportunities. Emotions are not the "truth," nor are they static. Rather, they change like the weather. Emotions urge us to action (emotion-driven behaviors). Sometimes those actions help us, but often they're not a good fit for the situation, get us into trouble, or result in chronic suffering. Emotions, even intensely distressing ones, are a part of being a living, breathing human being. You cannot escape them, and once they arrive, you can't make them go away. But the good news is that you can choose how you respond to them. Instead of acting on them, or fearing them, you can think of them as signals from the body and the brain, as one piece of information that might be useful, along with other kinds of awareness.

Processes That Reduce Emotion Avoidance and Overcontrol

If you're here, your scores indicate that emotion avoidance or overcontrol might be your go-to response across many stressful situations, and that it might be backfiring. If you stick with that strategy over all others, you might not be able to identify or express emotions when it would be helpful to do so, such as in an important relationship, or privately to yourself to understand what you want or need. And avoidance is likely making your feelings more intense and longer lasting. The average emotion lasts seven minutes at most (McKay and West 2016), but suppression or avoidance can extend an emotional wave indefinitely.

A more flexible approach allows you to observe your emotions. Then you can choose when you need to fully feel and express them, or when you might need to self-soothe or self-regulate, without shutting yourself down entirely. This will pave the way toward emotion acceptance, a superpower that allows you to validate your own internal experiences of the world, your own responses, and still choose when and where to express or share those experiences with others.

Watching and Allowing the Four Parts of an Emotion

The experience we call "emotion" is made up of physical processes in our nervous system that our brains then interpret, given our culture and our current context, as a specific emotion. This is done in a quick, delicate dance of thoughts, physical sensations, action urges, and language.

This exercise helps you practice paying attention to the components of an emotional experience, even if they're fleeting or hard to describe. This is best done when you have some time and space to yourself, and while you're already feeling some kind of emotion. We recommend that you read through these instructions right now, and then look back over them again, slowly, as you practice for the first time. Another option is recording and listening to them on your smartphone. We encourage you to practice *watching and allowing emotions* daily, if possible, but a minimum of three times a week.

If you're feeling a high-energy emotion, such as fear, anger, joy, or shame, you might do this practice sitting back or even lying on your back with your hand on your chest. If you're feeling a lower-energy emotion, like sadness, calmness, or boredom, you might try this exercise sitting upright, or even standing or walking.

You're going to pay attention to the four parts of this emotion you're feeling. It's okay if you have only the wisp of an emotion to work on, and it's okay if you think your emotion is "too much." The key is just to pay attention and keep breathing. There's no right or wrong way to do this. It's okay if your mind wanders away, and wanders back. Just do your best, and stay curious.

Physical Sensations:

Take a deep breath with your hand on your chest. Using the touch of your hand as a starting point, start to let your awareness spread to your entire body. Begin to note the different sensations you feel in your body, without thinking of them as "good" or "bad," or thinking of ways to fix them. There's no particular order—just notice whatever sensations jump into your mind. You might notice the pace of your breath or heart, you might notice muscle tension or shaking, you might notice tingling or flushed or heavy sensations. Pay attention to heat or coldness. Pay attention to clenching or "melting" feelings. Notice what your face is feeling, your shoulders, your gut. Notice your hands, your legs, your feet. Keep breathing with every new sensation, giving yourself permission to feel it fully, noticing if it is steady, or increasing, or shifting in some way. You might even imagine saying "okay" to each sensation, breathing in and growing to make space for it, and breathing out and relaxing into it.

Urges:

Keep breathing and notice if the sensations you're aware of come with any urges to do something. Anger might come with an urge to shout or strike out; fear might come with an urge to withdraw or hide; sadness might come with an urge to curl up, or to cry. You might have an urge to do all those things, or none, or something else. See if you can explore your own urges—let your mind really imagine what you might like to act on right now. There's no right or wrong answer. Keep breathing, and also notice what it is like to both *feel* an urge, and to *not be acting on it*. Does it come with a sense of tension, or excitement, or confusion? Welcome all of those. Notice if the urges swell and retreat, or if they're relatively stable.

Thoughts:

Now start to pay attention to any contents of your mind. You might have thoughts that are like sentences: *I never do anything right. I hate this. This is fun.* You might have thoughts that are more like flashes of images, or a confusing combination. Just let yourself observe these different goings-on of your mind without trying to figure them out, control them, or judge them as good or bad, true or untrue. Keep breathing, and just notice each thought as it comes and goes from your mind.

Emotion Label:

Now, take a few more breaths, and see what happens when you combine the experiences of sensation, urge, and thought. It might be a confusing, kaleidoscopic combination, or it might be a very clear picture of one particular emotion. Just stay curious, and see what it's like to pay attention to the bigger picture, the whole of these experiences. After a few moments of doing that, see if you can think of an emotion word or three that *might* describe what you're feeling. Depending on the languages you know, different possibilities might pop into your head for how to describe this whole experience. "Irritable." "Bored." "Overwhelmed." "Forlorn." "Scared." "Keyed-up." "Verklempt." You're not looking for the "right" answer—in fact, when you feel any emotion, there's no "right" emotion you're "really" feeling. Any number of words might be used to describe your experience. Just pick out a few that are a good enough fit. Imagine holding them lightly—emotions can shift and blend, so the words you use might need to shift, too.

To bring the exercise to a close, imagine cupping your chosen emotion word(s) in the palm of your hand, lightly, gently, and with curiosity, like you might hold a very interesting plant or rock you found. Breathe as you hold it, and even if it feels silly, *pretend* or *imagine* you are really enjoying the experience of your emotion: the shifting sensations, urges, and thoughts—even if it's an extremely strong "negative" emotion, such as grief, or rage. Pretend to cherish the experience, like you might cherish finding a beautiful wildflower or hidden stream.

To help you identify emotions, here is a list of English feeling words. But don't limit yourself. You can use color words, texture words, any number of creative ways to explain your experience to yourself.

Happy	Upset	Angry	Afraid
Peaceful	Devastated	Enraged	Scared
Content	Lonely	Irritated	Worried
Proud	Vulnerable	Judgmental	Anxious
Curious	Despairing	Appalled	Helpless
Playful	Guilty	Frustrated	Frightened
Inspired	Down	Critical	Nervous
Thankful	Hurt	Distant	Exposed
Sensitive	Worthless	Bitter	Rejected
Creative	Empty	Jealous	Threatened
Confident	Remorseful	Furious	Terrified
Inquisitive	Embarrassed	Violated	Fragile
Silly	Ashamed	Resentful	Pressured
Aroused	Alone	Annoyed	Overwhelmed
Excited	Disappointed	Withdrawn	Hesitant
Joyful	Disengaged	Infuriated	Stressed
Free	Apathetic	Skeptical	Shocked
Amazed	Overwhelmed	Impatient	Frozen

Each time you *watch and allow,* journal the four parts of your emotion in the following Emotion Record Worksheet. Keep documenting these emotional components until you have enough practice that they're easy to recognize.

Emotion Record Worksheet

Physical Sensations:

Urges:

Thoughts:

Emotion Words:

Example. Take a look at a one-day sample of Raj's Emotion Record Worksheet.

First Emotion

Physical Sensations: Forehead tight, arms tight, chest hot.

Urges: Hit something or run away.

Thoughts: She's baiting me. She's trying to make me look stupid. No one has my back.

Emotions: Anger. Sadness; a feeling that something's wrong with me.

Second Emotion

Physical Sensations: Heaviness in my body. Lethargy. Rooted in the chair.

Urges: Do nothing. Give up; let events take their course.

Thoughts: Nothing I do works. I'm alone. No one cares.

Emotions: Sadness. A feeling of letting go. Resigned.

Over many episodes of watching and allowing, Raj's Emotion Record Worksheet captured many of his feelings and their components. What he learned from watching and allowing is:

- Emotions come and go. No matter how intense, they don't last. Something always comes along to replace them.

- When you learn to watch emotions, you don't necessarily have to avoid them.

- "An urge is just an urge." It doesn't mean you have to do it.

Visiting Emotions

This exercise can help you build willingness, tolerance, and even interest in your emotions, both strong and subtle, both "negative" and "positive." It will also help you practice staying on the lookout for times when you might have an interesting emotion to observe—this will help you see emotional moments as opportunities, rather than as threats or problems to be fixed.

Take a deep breath. Close your eyes if you feel comfortable with that, or else let your gaze settle on something that's holding still, like the floor or a wall.

1. Think of a memory connected to the feeling of silliness, fun, or joy. Whatever pops into mind first is probably what you should go with. Give yourself several minutes to think about the memory—the smells, the sounds, the sights. Where were you, who else might have been there, what did you notice? It's okay to embellish the details a little if you don't remember—this is one part imagination, one part memory. Now take a deep breath and imagine you are there. Imagine how your body would feel experiencing the sensation of "fun" or "silliness." Let your body express that emotion—you might shift your facial expression, or notice some sensation in your muscles. No need to force, but whatever is happening, spend a few minutes observing it.

2. Now think of a memory connected to the feeling of sadness, or even grief. Again, whatever pops into mind first is probably what you should go with, and you can use any combination of memory and imagination that feels right to put yourself in a "scene" of sadness. Just like above, explore the sights, sounds, smells, and sensations of the memory. Let sadness fill you, let your body express it. Spend a few minutes here.

3. Now think of a memory connected to the feeling of anger, frustration, or irritation. Let your imagination take you into the scene, and feel whatever there is to feel there. Spend a few minutes in this experience.

Now open your eyes and return to the situation you are in at the moment. Notice what it was like to "call up" or "visit" those three different emotions—how your mind and body interacted to create the experience. Notice how long it took to switch, and what it's like now to sit quietly and let the emotions ramp back down. It will be different for everyone, so just be curious how it works for you. Do the emotions fade quickly? Do they stick around a few more seconds or minutes after you "turn off" the scene? How do you know? What signals in your body and mind tell you that?

Doing this exercise in moments when you're feeling relatively calm can help you practice noticing the onset and the departure of emotions and make some peace with how they come and go. It will also help your brain learn that moving in and out of even *very strong* emotions is not permanent, and not dangerous.

Imagery-Based Emotion Exposure

Situations occur throughout the week that stir your emotions—some that you don't want to feel. You try to push them away, but one of two things happens: (1) the emotions go into simmer mode, only to erupt later, or (2) your attempt to avoid heats the emotion to a new level of intensity. Imagery-based emotion exposure can teach you to have and hold emotions so they don't overwhelm you or erupt into negative, emotion-driven behavior.

Having an emotion is entirely different from acting on an emotion. Emotion-driven urges (attack, withdrawal, running away) put you under the control of your emotions. Learning to simply have and observe your feelings via emotion exposure teaches you to let emotions come and go without (1) resisting them or (2) acting on them with emotion-driven urges.

Any recent situation that stirred painful emotions is a good candidate for imagery-based emotion exposure. Here's what you do:

Visualize the past scene, trying to watch it as you would a video. What are you doing and saying? What are others doing and saying? See the setting where the event takes place. Notice your thoughts. Watch the scene unfold until you feel a significant physical or emotional reaction. (Somewhere between 5 and 7 on a 10-point scale.) This is the exposure.

Now shut off the scene and observe what's happening inside. Notice your body first, observing and allowing any physical sensation. Try to name what you feel.

Now try to observe and name any emotion that goes with the feeling in your body. Watch it for a few moments to see if you can learn more. Is it changing as you watch—either its intensity or perhaps morphing or blending into other emotions?

Notice any thoughts, but don't get involved with them. Just label them ("sad thought"… "anger thought"…"fear thought"…"shame thought"—whatever they are) and let them go.

Notice urges—either to avoid or do some emotion-driven behavior. Observe what it's like to feel the urge but not act on it.

Now return to:

observing sensations in your body, naming them, and noticing if they are changing

observing emotions, naming them, and noticing if they are changing

observing, labeling, and letting go of any thoughts

observing urges

Cycle through sensations, emotions, thoughts, and urges two more times.

Reflect at the end of imagery-based emotion exposure. What did you learn about the emotion? Were you able to have and hold it without avoiding? How did the emotion change as you watched?

Use emotion exposure each time you have an upsetting experience so you can learn to observe and tolerate the feeling—without avoiding or engaging in emotion-driven behavior.

Example. Julia faced a difficult moment when her boss asked her to explain a recent workflow issue. Her immediate response was to be crushed and feel a sinking sense of failure. She tersely ended the conversation and walked out of her boss's office. That evening, sitting in a quiet space at home, Julia did an exposure following the steps of the process:

> She visualized her boss's office and what was said. She watched the scene unfold, observing both her emotions and how they felt in her body. She noticed the "failure" thoughts that came up until her distress reaction was about 6 on the 10-point scale.

> Julia shut the scene off. She noticed the feelings in her body—a heavy sensation in her stomach; a tingling, "disaster" feeling in her spine. At first the sensation seemed hard to describe, but as she watched, the words came to her.

> The emotion was harder to locate. Tiredness? No. It felt deeper than that. A bad feeling about herself? Not exactly. It felt more like sinking, a sadness. She watched the sadness, noticing a sense of wanting to give up. As Julia observed the feeling, she experienced the sadness shifting into loss, a feeling that she would never be valued by her supervisor.

> Julia's thoughts seemed mostly to be self-attacks: *I'm screwing up…bad…she's done with me.* For each thought, she noticed what it was—another judgment about herself—and let it go, returning to observe her body and emotions.

> The urge was to give up, quit. She felt the pull of it—to say "F-you" to her boss and walk out. And she observed what it was like to sit without acting.

> She returned to observing that experience, sitting with sensations, emotions, and urges.

> Julia cycled through sensations, emotions, thoughts, and urges a number of times, noticing how her emotion (sadness) changed in intensity and morphed into something that felt more like "whatever."

> After the exposure she noticed that an emotion that seemed overwhelming became something she could stand, something she could watch without trying to escape. She also was surprised to see the sadness downshift into something softer—almost peace.

Processes That Increase Emotion Acceptance

You've been working up until now to reduce emotion avoidance, knowing how it serves to increase emotion intensity, duration, and the tendency to emotion-driven behaviors. The following processes will *increase* emotion acceptance and an openness to feeling whatever comes up for you.

Exploring Your Emotional Landscape

This process uses visualization and metaphor to help you get curious and nonjudgmental about your inner emotional landscape. This exercise is best done when you *aren't* already feeling completely overwhelmed by a strong emotion. If you're feeling overwhelmed, you might want to utilize chapter 4: Resilience.

Get out a piece of paper and something to write with. If you have crayons or colored pencils, even better.

Without trying to get it exactly "right" (you can always try this exercise multiple times), start to draw what your strongest, most frequent emotions might look like if they were on a map of your mind. You might make a lake of anger-lava around the rage volcano, which then feeds into the rocky terrain of self-doubt. You might have a forest of uncertainty and terror, maybe in the center, or off to the side, or a sparkling river of delight that moves across the whole landscape. You might notice a desert of boredom, with an oasis of daydreaming. Your landscape might have a giant pit of despair, or mountain of grief. Get as creative as you want, but don't worry about being creative "enough." You could even just draw a lot of circles if you want. The point is just to get a little silly and loose with it.

Remember, none of these geological features of your emotional landscape are good or bad, right or wrong to have. Each one of us contains a whole world.

Next time you feel a strong emotion, you might even close your eyes for a moment and picture yourself surfing over the lava-moat, or wandering around your forest of terror.

Sharing Your Emotional Language

One of the most beautiful things about showing up as your full, emotional self is that it gives those around you permission to do so, as well. You can plant a seed with your closest loved ones that grows into a garden within your whole community—a garden where vulnerability, honesty, and self-expression are cherished.

One way of doing that is sharing your way of putting language to your emotional experiences. Here are three steps you can practice:

Step 1: Practice saying emotions out loud to yourself.

Sometimes putting voice to emotions can feel awkward. A good way to get your mind really comfortable with doing this is to "share" your feelings with yourself. Over the course of the next week, try to say your feelings out loud to yourself at least three times a day. So you might drop a glass, and say to yourself, "Well, I'm feeling surprised and pissed off." You might open your email, notice a flutter in your stomach, and say, "I wonder if I'm nervous or excited." You might be in the shower and note to yourself, "Today I felt a lot of different things: I was bored, I was frustrated, I was satisfied. Right now I'm drowsy."

Step 2: Practice saying what you feel to trusted or safe loved ones.

The next step is to use emotion words more often in your closest relationships. You might note to your partner, "Huh, I think I might be irritated right now. I'm definitely frustrated." Or you might put your hand on your heart while you're talking to your sibling and say, "I might be sad, maybe?" You might say to your dear friend on the phone, "I feel sort of safe and content, listening to you." Notice that you leave a little room for nuance—you're holding your emotion words lightly, but you're also offering them to the person close to you, to share your experience as best you can. The great thing about this practice is that you might get some of these gems back, and get to learn more about the inner workings of others' minds, too.

Step 3: Practice saying emotions in situations where you're not sure you're "allowed" to.

This is a next level emotion-expression maneuver, and you need to be willing to take a bit of a risk. See if you can find three places in the next week to use an emotion word outside your very safest bubble of relationships. It might be with someone who's "close" to you, but the relationship feels fraught. You might say, "You know what, I think I'm feeling cautious right now." Or you might say to a stranger, "Hey, I'm feeling a bit uncomfortable." Or you might note in a meeting, "Hey, gotta be honest, I'm feeling a little touchy about this."

As you start to explore lightly sharing your experiences, you'll find how others react. As you gain more and more strength in emotion acceptance and openness, you might find that it's really important to you that your relationships have openness, too. As you test the waters and run these little experiments, you collect useful information about which relationships can and can't handle this kind of talk. Does your partner express their feelings back and remain interested in your experiences? Does your boss nod and validate your worry? Does your friend try to talk you out of whatever feeling you're having? Does your parent outright tell you what to feel? Do you get apologies, sharing, validation, or contradiction, or are you ignored? Some combination? All of this information might help guide where you put your emotional energy, where you let yourself be the most vulnerable, and where you might want to shift, scale back, or end some relationships that aren't in line with your values and strengths.

Emotion-Acceptance Meditation

Record the following emotion-acceptance meditation on your smartphone and listen once a day.

Close your eyes and focus on your breath. Notice the place where your breath starts, the center of your breath and life. Say to yourself, "In" on the in-breath and "Out" on the out-breath. (*Pause*) In and out. (*Pause*)

When thoughts arise, just say to yourself, "Thought," and return to your breath. (*Pause*) In and out. (*Pause*)

Notice any sensations in your body—just scan your body from head to toe. (*Pause*) Some feelings may be pleasant; some uncomfortable. Just try to notice each feeling in your body without judgment. (*Pause*) Make room for each feeling, allowing it to be there. (*Pause*)

Now notice the part of you that feels in an emotional way. And notice the particular emotion you feel at this moment. (*Pause*) Be aware if it feels good or not so good. And allow it to be whatever it is. See if you can accept this feeling without judgment. (*Pause*) Let the feeling be as it is, or change. Make room for it to be and do what it wants. (*Pause*) If another emotion should arise or the first one change, let the new feeling be as it is. (*Pause*) Just watching and allowing this emotion to be what it is. (*Pause*) Accepting this emotion without judging or resisting it. Opening to it. Permitting it to have this moment in your life. (*Pause*)

And now take a breath. Breathe in this emotion and breathe out acceptance. (*Pause*) Breathe in the emotion and breathe out acceptance. You can have this feeling right now. Allow yourself to name it. Once more, breathe it in and breathe out acceptance. Allowing. Allowing. Allowing.

And when you're ready, take one more breath and end the meditation.

Summary

In this chapter you have learned to accept your strong emotions with openness and curiosity, without trying to avoid strong feelings. You've done this in two ways: (1) learning to reduce emotion avoidance and overcontrol and (2) increasing your openness to your emotional experiences, including expressing your emotions to others.

From here, return to the assessment chapter and look at your next highest scores on the Comprehensive Coping Inventory–55. That will tell you which chapter to work on next.

CHAPTER 6

Peace: From Thought Avoidance to Thought Acceptance

You have turned to this chapter because you scored high on section 6 of the Comprehensive Coping Inventory–55, "Thought Avoidance," meaning that you often try to replace or suppress distressing thoughts. This is one way your mind is always trying to protect you and help you survive every single moment. But it does so in ways that sometimes backfire and create emotional pain. In this chapter you'll learn processes to work with your mind and all of its incredible capacities without letting it "protect" you in ways that harm you. And in the process you'll create a sense of peace in your day-to-day life.

Thought Avoidance: What It Is

One of the unfortunate things your mind does is try to push away, replace, or stop your thinking when you're having uncomfortable thoughts. This process is called *thought avoidance,* or, technically, *cognitive avoidance.* Let's look at how thought avoidance plays out in some hypothetical scenarios:

- You experienced a difficult childhood, and your memories from this period get triggered at times. You try to replace the upsetting memories with a positive one, such as the last vacation you took, or distract yourself by checking Facebook. But the more you push them away, the more insistent and painful the memories become.

- You're eager to apply for a promotion at work. When hearing about a job opening, you get excited since it's a position you've been waiting to apply for. Then you think, *I probably won't get it anyway. What if I make a fool of myself? Would I be a good leader?* To manage these negative thoughts, you decide to eat a burger to distract yourself, so you place an order right away. But when you've had the last bite, the thoughts come back—with a vengeance. The more you try to get rid of them, the more you seem to fill with self-doubt and the expectation of failure.

- Your kids are traveling to South America, and you have a thought about something bad happening to them on the trip. Then you're telling yourself to stop thinking that horrible thought. But it comes back, and the more you try to banish the thought, the more haunted and fearful you become.

In these examples, you do everything you can not to think about something uncomfortable. You try to get rid of, minimize, replace, or suppress those thoughts. But here's the problem with cognitive avoidance: the more you try to block painful thoughts, the more often they show up and the more persistent and "sticky" they become. As their frequency and intensity increase, so does the emotional pain your thoughts trigger.

The way to heal from this emotional pain is to move from thought avoidance to thought acceptance—the capacity to let thoughts come and go without resisting or getting attached to them. Although the skills are intertwined, we'll break this down into two parts, focusing first on ways to decrease avoidance and then on exercises to increase acceptance.

Processes That Reduce Thought Avoidance

Here is the path forward: learning to have all those thoughts—the scary, old, and ugly ones—without blocking, avoiding, or pushing them down. You don't have to approve of or like all the thoughts your mind generates. But you can learn to make room for these thoughts as they are and to look at them as stuff your mind comes up with rather than as thoughts you always have to take seriously.

You can start watching your mind and all the content it generates by practicing two key processes: mindfulness of the mind and cognitive exposure.

Mindfulness of the Mind

Mindfulness is the process of observing your experience in a nonjudgmental, compassionate, and accepting manner. It begins with simple awareness, paying attention to your experience from moment to moment. As you practice mindfulness, you will learn that your thoughts come and go. The more you practice, the more you'll learn to step back and notice this process as an impartial observer, rather than responding to negative thoughts by avoiding or getting caught in them. You'll learn to allow them without being very concerned about them or even finding them important. Your life can then be about the things that matter to you instead of fighting and losing battles with your mind.

In multiple clinical studies, mindfulness has been shown to significantly reduce anxiety, depression, stress (Astin, 1997), and rumination (Chambers, Lo, and Allen 2008); facilitate the management of chronic pain (Kabat-Zinn et al. 1995); improve cognitive flexibility (Davidson et al. 2003), compassion (Shapiro and Schwartz 2000), and physical functioning (Davidson et al. 2003); and enhance overall well-being.

Mindfulness, as a skill, will help you do three things:

1. notice your thoughts without running away from them;

2. focus your attention on the present moment, rather than getting caught in all the thoughts that your mind generates; and

3. build the capacity to make choices based on your values, not on your thoughts.

Spending a lot of your time, effort, and energy on getting rid of your thoughts only intensifies the pain, struggle, and discomfort that come with them. It may not feel so bad when you're in the midst of avoiding thoughts, but it's quite likely that even though avoidance works for a moment, it's only a matter of time until your mind again comes up with the same, similar, or even worse thoughts.

The bottom line is this: learning to accept your thoughts for what they are and staying in the present moment is an antidote to the thoughts that get you in trouble.

Remember that wherever you go, your mind won't stop trying to protect you; it's like a security device that is on 24/7, with no vacation, no holidays, and no breaks. So instead of wrestling and resisting those unwanted thoughts and all the noise that your mind makes, it's helpful to learn to navigate life *while* having all that mind noise.

Here's a mini-exercise to understand how suppressing your thoughts makes them more persistent and frequent. First, read the directions for this exercise all the way through. Next, set a timer for 1 minute for each step. Then put this book down and follow the steps.

1. Do your best not to think about carrots for 1 minute. You read that right! For 60 seconds, put all your effort into not thinking about carrots.

2. Now, for 60 seconds, make sure you don't think about anything related to carrots, broccoli, or zucchini. Try to prevent any thought of those vegetables from entering your mind.

3. For 60 seconds, erase any memory, image, or thought related to carrots. Really do your best to make any image related to carrots disappear.

What did you observe? Could you banish all thoughts of carrots? As much as you try to control your thoughts, like with the exercise above, you also must face reality: you don't have control of what shows up in your mind, when it shows up, or how it shows up. And the more you try to stop a particular thought, *the more you have it.* When you try to block a thought, you're doing the impossible. So the more you try to get rid of those uncomfortable, annoying, or painful thoughts, images, and memories, the more you're adding logs to the fire. Rather than getting rid of them, you're actually opening a mental doorway for those thoughts to bombard you.

Instead of focusing on whether a thought is true or false, positive or negative, accurate or not, it's more helpful to learn to notice your thoughts for what they are: an ongoing stream of content that your protective mind generates all the time. It's not your fault, it just happens that all humans have busy minds. One way to tackle your busy mind and shift from thought avoidance to thought acceptance is by practicing mindfulness.

The Basics of Mindfulness

Let's start with common misconceptions about mindfulness:

- Practicing mindfulness doesn't mean that you have to have a serious facial expression, keep your eyes closed all the time, or force yourself to look peaceful. Practicing mindfulness is a very individualized activity that, by its very nature, shifts from moment to moment—because every moment that we're alive is different. Sometimes you may have a peaceful expression, other times a poker face or even a frown; there are no rules about having a "mindful" face.

- Mindfulness, as you'll learn it here, isn't a thought vacuum. Practicing mindfulness in your daily life is a skill of paying attention in the moment to whatever shows up without trying to change anything. It means letting your thoughts, memories, and images simply be, even if they're distressing. Mindfulness is observing—the opposite of resisting.

- You don't need to be relaxed to practice mindfulness. It's natural that you would want to be stress-free and as calm as possible. It's understandable that you're attracted to anything that may give you a sense of peace. But the purpose of mindfulness is not about being relaxed or mellow. If you experience some form of relaxation, that's definitely a plus, but not the goal.

The following exercise will help you to strengthen your ability to watch your mind without struggling, avoiding, or resisting thoughts, memories, or images that may come your way.

Watching Your Mind Mindfully

You can choose to record the directions below and play them back, or simply read them and practice the exercise.

Close your eyes and take a deep breath. Notice the experience of breathing as it's happening; notice every time you're inhaling and exhaling. Watch the air as it passes through your nose. Notice the sensation of your ribs expanding, the air entering your lungs, how your diaphragm moves with every breath. Notice the sensation of releasing the air as you exhale. (*Pause*)

Just keep watching your breath, letting your attention move along the path of flowing air...in and out...in and out...watching your breath. Imagine that you're watching a door opening and closing with every breath. (*Pause*)

As you breathe, you will also notice other experiences. You may watch thoughts coming and going; when a thought comes up, just say to yourself, "Thought." Just label it for what it is: thought. Try not to hold onto any of the thoughts. Just label them one by one and let them go. Let them go on your out-breath. Until the next thought comes. (*Pause*)

You are just watching your mind while labeling thoughts. If some of the thoughts are painful, uncomfortable, or annoying, do your best to notice and allow any emotions. As new thoughts arise, new feelings will, too. No need to argue back, dwell on, or entertain the thought. Just do your best to label it "thought." Let it go with your out-breath, and be open for the next one. (*Pause*)

Keep watching your thoughts as they come, one by one. Let them happen, let them be. Let them go on the out-breath. (*Pause*)

Your thoughts are all just weather, while you are the sky. Just passing weather...your task is to watch those thoughts, label them, and let them go. No need to resist them or hold onto them. Allow your thoughts and let them go. Allow your feelings, and let them change and evolve. Allowing and letting go. (*Pause*)

Finish this exercise by taking five deep breaths, as you transition from watching your mind to returning to your day.

Practice this mindful exercise twice daily.

Example. Raphael used the Watching Your Mind Mindfully exercise and discovered several habitual thoughts that kept coming to the surface:

- images of parts of his body with the thought "bad"

- memories of his father raging at him

- a sense of failure in his marriage with memories of specific criticisms from his wife

- the image of punching his wife—something he had never done and hated himself for having in his mind

During the first week practicing this mind-watching exercise, Raphael noticed something important: allowing and labeling his thoughts, rather than resisting and trying to banish them, reduced their frequency. The disturbing thoughts showed up less often, and when they did were easier to let go of. Whether it was memories of his father raging or images of punching his wife, Raphael allowed the thought, labeled it ("It's just a thought"), and let it go with his out-breath. *Notice and allow, label, and let go with the breath* was the sequence he followed with each thought, no matter how painful or disturbing.

As Raphael continued mind watching over many weeks, two other changes began to take root. First, the thoughts seemed to have less and less power to trigger a painful emotion. All of Raphael's most disturbing thoughts generated shame, but over weeks of allowing and labeling them as "just thoughts," Raphael began to believe it. They were just "things in his mind," as opposed to some deep truth about his worth as a human being.

The second outcome was that Raphael started to *notice and allow, label, and let go with the breath* throughout the day—not just during his practice sessions. It started to get almost automatic and forged a new relationship with his old disturbing thoughts.

Cognitive Exposure

Another way to reduce thought avoidance is by intentionally focusing your attention on a painful, unwanted thought, memory, or image that you usually try to avoid—a process known as *cognitive exposure*. The process of turning toward rather than away from the thought, memory, or image will make it (1) less frequent, (2) less painful, and (3) less important. Note that in this exercise, the word "thought" refers to any thought, memory, or image. Begin by listing on the following worksheet current painful or disturbing thoughts that you push away and resist.

Cognitive Exposure Worksheet

Painful/Disturbing Thoughts That You Try to Resist	Exposures (Urge to Avoid Rated 0–10)				
	1	2	3	4	5
1.					
2.					
3.					
4.					
5.					
6.					
7.					
8.					
9.					
10.					

To conduct a cognitive exposure, find a quiet place and schedule 10 to 15 minutes of your time; it's helpful if you have a device to prerecord yourself reading the directions slowly and in a soft voice. Then listen to your recording and follow the directions.

Get into a comfortable position. Close your eyes or focus your gaze on a single point, then take a few slow, deep breaths. Allow yourself some moments to get centered. (*Pause*)

Now get in touch with a thought from your list that you usually run away from, try to get rid of, or avoid at all costs. Let's call this your target thought. While focusing on this thought, do your best to stay in touch with feelings and any other reactions that come along. Do your best to watch how your body responds. (*Pause*) Do you notice any urges to suppress, eliminate, or push away the thought? How intense are the urges? Are they mild, moderate, or intense? (*Pause*)

Notice where the urge to get rid of this thought begins and ends. Notice exactly where it is in your body. If you could make a sculpture in the shape of this urge, what would it look like? Observe whether this urge is pushing you to suppress your target thought, or distract yourself from it. (*Pause*)

After noticing the urges that come with the target thought, see if you can completely "drop the battle" and stop the fight by simply noticing and observing the thought. Describe the thought, memory, or image to yourself silently without doing anything about it. (*Pause*)

What if, instead of fighting against the thought, you chose to have it, exactly as it is? If you are still resisting, do your best again to just drop the battle, drop the fight against the thought. (*Pause*)

Notice what comes when you drop the fight against the thought. See what happens if you choose to have this particular thought. You don't have to like it or dislike it; you don't have to love it; you don't have to deny it. You just have to do your best to let it be as it is. (*Pause*)

As you drop the fight with this thought, see if you can get in contact with the person behind your eyes, the person having this experience. Let's call the person "the observer you." See if you can notice the observer you that is watching this thought, memory, or image, and is watching your mind have it. What do you notice? (*Pause*)

Now, from the place of looking at that thought and having it, see what it feels like to notice the pull to take action, without actually taking action. (*Pause*)

Now ask yourself, *Is there anything in this thought that I cannot have or that could hurt me?* (*Pause*)

Notice how it is to unpack this thought: what it does, how it feels, and how you can have it without doing anything. Reflect for several moments on these questions. (*Pause*)

As you prepare to finish this exercise, notice your breathing. Take a few good, deep breaths with the air coming in through your nose and out through your mouth. Gently open your eyes and bring yourself back to the room.

Now, on the Cognitive Exposure Worksheet, rate the thought from 0 to 10 in terms of how strong the urge is to avoid it.

As you move forward, ask yourself, *Am I willing to go on from here, carrying all these thoughts wherever I go? Allowing them to arise without resisting or holding onto them?*

Repeat this cognitive exposure exercise twice daily, focusing each time on a thought/memory/image you've recently been resisting (and is listed on your Cognitive Exposure Worksheet).

Example. Lorie struggled with six distressing thoughts that she hated and kept trying to suppress. Some of them related to memories of a sexual assault and ideas that she was broken. One recurring thought focused on a kind of sexual behavior that she found both attractive and abhorrent. Below is her worksheet.

Painful/Disturbing Thoughts That You Try to Resist	Exposures				
	(Urge to Avoid Rated 0–10)				
	1	2	3	4	5
1. The feeling of being pushed down, controlled.	9	9	7	5	
2. His hand over my mouth to keep me from screaming.	8	6	7	4	4
3. The thought of X sexual experience: excited and disgusted.	9	8	8	6	5
4. The thought: I'm worthless, broken.	7	6	5	6	4
5. The thought: No one will want or love me.	7	6	6	6	5
6. The thought that God let this happen—doesn't care.	10	8	5	6	3

Lorie didn't complete the exposures to the thoughts in order, but rather chose one from the list that intuitively felt important to work on. She listened to the taped exposure process for the chosen thought, determined to observe and stay with the thought for the entire length of the recording.

At the end of each exposure, Lorie rated her urge to avoid the thought. She repeated the exposures for each thought until she could tolerate the thought without having a strong urge to push it away. When she no longer felt a strong urge to avoid or block the thought, Lorie chose another thought to work on.

Processes That Increase Cognitive Acceptance

Cognitive acceptance comes from observing and allowing your mind to do what it does—think. It helps you accept any thought, regardless of veracity, regardless of its emotional valence. In this section we'll focus on two processes to cultivate cognitive acceptance, beginning with journaling.

Journaling with Purpose

Journaling with purpose allows you to identify the function of your thoughts, see their value, and accept all products of your mind. Here is what you need to do.

Find a quiet place to journal so you won't be bothered. Next, think about a challenging situation you recently experienced; it could be an upsetting moment at work, in your relationships, or in your career. Do your best to choose a moment of struggle that you want to unpack and learn from.

Once you have decided on the situation, write about it, doing your best to include all the details. Try to capture the uniqueness of that particular moment so you can see it, hear it, feel it, and live it.

Next, write down all the thoughts that show up in your mind. Try to capture each of them the best you can. Circle the ones that are more troublesome to you. When examining those thoughts and circling them, it's possible you may see a theme among them. If so, select the sentence that captures the theme, and keep your eyes open for other themes. It's okay if you don't see a theme; not everyone will.

After circling those words, ask yourself the following questions and respond to them in your journal. Slow down a bit when considering these questions so you give yourself a chance to reflect, learn, and continue to cultivate awareness of thoughts.

- Why does this thought hurt so much?

- What's the struggle, pain, or difficulty this thought is conveying to me?

- What is this thought trying to teach me?

- Is this thought trying to protect me from something? Is it working?

- Is there any value hidden in this thought?

- Is there anything I care deeply about that this thought reflects?

- What is this thought suggesting I do?

- Is this thought influencing my behavior? Do I want that?

- Do I need this thought?

- How do I want to live my life in the face of this thought?

Practicing this exercise and journaling with purpose will increase your ability to watch your mind, hold your thoughts lightly, and learn about the function of your most distressing cognitions. Set time aside after any upsetting event to journal with purpose so you can learn about and begin to accept how your mind responds.

Example. Julie chose an incident with her son for the focus of her journaling exercise. She described the situation in this way:

"I'm calling him to come in from playing to do his homework. He doesn't seem to hear me and goes on playing. I'm feeling tense. I think he's got to get started or we'll be up all night trying to get it done. I shout louder and he actually moves away—farther down the block. I'm leaning out the window, calling and calling, and he's riding his scooter down the hill. Finally, I run outside, feeling so angry, and grab him by the arm. He's screeching, 'Don't, don't,' as I pull him into the house. I slam his books on the dining room table and shout for him to get started. He's crying, saying I'm mean."

Thoughts that Julie circled:

He doesn't listen.

I'm a bad mother.

I can't control my child.

There's something wrong with me—my anger.

He has no discipline—he won't get anywhere in life.

The key themes were:

1.   I'm a bad mother because of my anger.

2.   There's something wrong with my boy; he has no inner discipline.

This is how Julie explored the "bad mother" theme:

- Why does this thought hurt so much? *Because being a good mom is so important to me.*

- What is the struggle, pain, or difficulty this thought is conveying to me? *I feel helpless to get him to mind me. I'm afraid he won't be disciplined enough to do well in school. And life.*

- What is this thought trying to teach me? *That I'm hurting him with my anger.*

- Is this thought trying to protect me from something? Is it working? *Maybe from failing as a mom. It doesn't help anything.*

- Is there any value hidden in this thought? *I want to be a loving, supportive mom. Not one who hurts her boy.*

- Is there anything I care deeply about that this thought reflects? *To be loving above all.*

- What is this thought suggesting I do? *Get help? Learn how to deal with misbehavior without anger?*

- Is this thought influencing my behavior? Do I want that? *No. It just makes me hate myself.*

- Do I need this thought? *Maybe. I need to face and change what I'm doing that hurts him.*

- How do I want to live my life in the face of this thought? *The thought is telling me I need to change. And when I push the thought away, I'm pushing away the truth.*

Julie, after journaling with purpose, decided to enroll in an online parent effectiveness course.

Rating Your Willingness

Another process designed to increase thought acceptance combines practicing mindfulness, recording your thoughts, and rating your willingness to allow them. This exercise begins by inviting you to watch your mind wandering and follow the thoughts as they morph, shift, and transform on their own.

Find a quiet place, grab a timer, and read the directions before proceeding with this exercise:

Set the timer for 10 minutes. Focus your gaze on a single point or close your eyes. Next, intentionally watch what your mind does. Every time you notice a thought show up, just watch it—without doing anything, without trying to solve anything. Intentionally watch what happens with those thoughts…let your attention wander, allow the next thought to be there…

Now, as you watch your wandering mind, write each thought (or as many as you can) on the Rating Your Willingness Worksheet below. As you record each thought, try to accept its presence in your mind. You might even use an affirmation, such as *I can allow this thought* or *I'm willing to have this thought.* Then, in the right-hand column, rate your willingness from 0 (totally unwilling to have the thought and any associated feelings) to 10 (completely willing to allow this thought and any related feelings).

Rating Your Willingness Worksheet

Wandering Mind Thoughts	Willingness (0–10)
1.	
2.	
3.	
4.	
5.	
6.	
7.	
8.	
9.	
10.	
11.	
12.	
13.	
14.	
15.	

Let's look at how Julie completed her Rating Your Willingness Worksheet. As Julie's mind shifted from thought to thought, she paused to write each one down. Some were so fast and fleeting, she couldn't catch them. But she was able to note many of the bigger, more noticeable cognitions. As she wrote and read each one, Julie said to herself, *I can allow this,* took a deep breath, and rated her willingness to have the thought. Here's some of what she experienced:

Wandering Mind Thoughts	Willingness (0–10)
1. I forgot to shop.	6
2. Josh (son) got a bad grade in math.	4
3. Vacation plan to Yosemite	10
4. Parent–teacher conference—what will happen?	7
5. Josh's teacher is too demanding.	7
6. Why can't we do better with his homework?	5
7. The car is making a knocking sound.	8
8. Will make the frozen pork chops tonight.	10
9. I'm sick of rice.	10
10. There's no rest.	6
11. Too many things in a day.	7
12. I'm not good at managing my time.	5
13. Josh isn't good at that either.	5
14. Josh still gives me sweet hugs.	10
15. I'm gaining weight.	4

Julie did the Rating Your Willingness exercise for 5 to 10 minutes daily. With practice, she found herself more and more able to observe her wandering thoughts with detachment and willingness. Even the painful thoughts about Josh could pass through her mind without resistance or a lot of distress. They were just thoughts, and she increasingly could allow her mind to have them.

One day, she said something to her son that surprised her: "I'll never stop worrying about you. And I'll never stop loving you." Somehow, she knew, that had come from acceptance of mind.

Summary

In this chapter you learned how to stop avoiding distressing thoughts and move toward acceptance—by observing your mind's monologue with openness and curiosity. Practicing mindfulness, cognitive exposure, journaling with purpose, and rating your willingness will allow you to focus on the present moment and be guided by your values rather than your thoughts—bringing a sense of peace to your life.

From here, return to the assessment chapter and look at your next highest scores on the Comprehensive Coping Inventory–55. That will tell you which chapter to work on next.

CHAPTER 7

Clarity: From Cognitive Misappraisal to Flexible Thinking

Your score on section 7 of the Comprehensive Coping Inventory–55 indicates that you struggle with cognitive misappraisal. In some high-stress situations you tend to have inaccurate, negative thoughts that worsen the situation by making you feel depressed, anxious, or angry.

This chapter will help you gain clarity of mind—the ability to think clearly, make accurate judgments, and stay mentally flexible under stress. When you gain clarity, you see everything in your life more clearly. You can identify real threats and avoid them, take advantage of opportunities, improve your relationships, and handle daily stresses with grace and composure.

First you will work through exercises drawn from the past 50 years of research on cognitive behavioral psychology. You will learn change processes to uncover, analyze, and balance your automatic thoughts. Second, you will identify your flexible thinking skills and develop processes to broaden them into new areas of your life.

Cognitive Misappraisal: What It Is

The central concept of cognitive therapy is that thoughts cause feelings. It's a three-step process of event, thought, then feeling:

Event – You reach for your phone and it's not in your pocket or purse where you usually keep it.

Thought – You think, *Oh no, I've lost my phone. What a disaster, I can't be without my phone!*

Feeling – You feel anxious and angry at yourself.

It is your interpretation of the event, not the event itself, that causes the feeling. If you thought, *Oh yeah, my phone is on the kitchen counter,* your feelings would have been different, perhaps mild annoyance at your forgetfulness, or maybe relief that your phone is safe in your home.

Most distressing situations are not this simple. There is often a feedback loop in which an automatic thought itself becomes an "event" that you interpret with further negative thoughts, causing further bad feelings.

Cognitive misappraisal is this tendency to misinterpret events, typically in inflexible ways that result in difficult emotions.

Processes That Reduce Cognitive Misappraisal

Learning processes to examine your automatic thoughts will enable you to gain some clarity about the pattern cognitive misappraisal in your own life and begin learning ways to reduce it. An extremely useful tool is the Thought Journal.

Recording Automatic Thoughts

Make some copies of the form below and carry them with you for a week. Whenever you experience painful emotions, write down in the first column the situation you were in. In the second column, write one word describing your bad feeling: *anxious, worried, nervous, angry, irritated, sad, disappointed, depressed,* and so on. Rate the feeling from 0 to 100, with 0 being no discomfort at all and 100 being the most painful negative feeling possible. In the third column, write down whatever was going through your mind before and while you were having the feeling. (We'll get to the last two columns soon.)

Thought Journal

Situation *When? Where? Who? What happened?*	Feelings *One-word summaries Rate 0–100*	Automatic Thoughts *What you were thinking just before and during the unpleasant feeling*	Limited Thinking Pattern	Balancing or Alternative Thoughts *Underline possible action plans*

Example. Janice was a mother of two school-age children. She and her husband ran a struggling motel in a small southwestern town. Her oldest son, Jimmy, had a severe learning disability. Here are some typical entries from Janice's Thought Journal.

Situation *When? Where? Who? What happened?*	Feelings *One-word summaries Rate 0–100*	Automatic Thoughts *What you were thinking just before and during the unpleasant feeling*	Limited Thinking Pattern	Balancing or Alternative Thoughts *Underline possible action plans*
Jimmy tore up his book report after we spent an hour on it.	Furious 70 Hopeless 50	Hates me. Does it on purpose to hurt me. He'll never make it in this world.		
2 air conditioners died the same day. Another one is barely working.	Worried 90	Already owe the HVAC guy money. Can't afford new ones. We'll lose this place.		
Husband buys three new AC units on credit card.	Angry 85	Fool. He'll ruin us. Homeless. We'll lose the business.		

Janice's automatic thoughts often came as single words or images, a kind of shorthand that she had to flesh out in her Thought Journal: She fleshed out "Hates me" to mean "He does it on purpose to hurt me." "Fool" started as an image of a foolish boy she knew in grade school, who ruined her eighth birthday party. Janice unpacked the single word "Homeless" to reveal her fear that "We'll lose the business."

Identifying Limited Thinking Patterns

After a week of keeping your Thought Journal, you will have recorded enough automatic thoughts to start identifying the limited thinking patterns that underly your cognitive misappraisals. *Limited thinking patterns* are habits of thought, ways of interpreting the world that you tend to fall back on in difficult situations. Here are the eight most common limited thinking patterns:

Filtering. You focus on the negative details while ignoring all the positive aspects of a situation.

Polarized Thinking. Things are black or white, good or bad. You have to be perfect or you're a failure. There's no middle ground, no room for mistakes.

Overgeneralization. You reach a general conclusion based on a single incident or piece of evidence. You exaggerate the frequency of problems and use negative global labels.

Mind Reading. Without their saying so, you know what people are feeling and why they act the way they do. In particular, you have certain knowledge of how people think and feel about you.

Catastrophizing. You expect disaster. You notice or hear about a problem and start asking, "What if?" What if tragedy strikes? What if it happens to you?

Magnifying. You exaggerate the degree or intensity of a problem. You turn up the volume on anything bad, making it loud, large, and overwhelming.

Personalization. You assume that everything people do or say is some kind of reaction to you. You also compare yourself to others, trying to determine who is smarter, more competent, better looking, and so on.

Shoulds. You have a list of ironclad rules about how you and other people should act. People who break the rules anger you, and you feel guilty when you violate the rules.

Now, in the fourth column of your Thought Journal, classify your automatic thoughts according to the eight limited thinking patterns. You can use situations that you've already recorded, and also add new situations as they come up. You'll probably find that you tend to use the same limited thinking patterns over and over, sometimes separately and sometimes combining them.

Take a look at how Janice completed the fourth column of her Thought Journal:

Situation *When? Where? Who? What happened?*	Feelings *One-word summaries Rate 0–100*	Automatic Thoughts *What you were thinking just before and during the unpleasant feeling*	Limited Thinking Pattern	Balancing or Alternative Thoughts *Underline possible action plans*
Jimmy tore up his book report after we spent an hour on it.	Furious 70 Hopeless 50	Hates me. Does it on purpose to hurt me. He'll never make it in this world.	Personalization Catastrophizing	
Husband buys three new AC units on credit card.	Angry 85	Fool. He'll ruin us. Homeless. We'll lose the business.	Catastrophizing	
Made Jimmy cry by pushing him too hard on his math problems.	Ashamed 70	I'm a failure as a mother. I'm blowing it.	Shoulds	
Loan officer at the bank kept me waiting, then rushed me, wouldn't let me finish a sentence.	Angry 50 Nervous 75	She can tell I'm desperate. She feels contempt and pity for us. She's supposed to help, not hinder.	Mind Reading Shoulds	

Supplying Alternative Thoughts

In the last column of your Thought Journal, make up some balancing or alternative thoughts that might apply to the situation. These are thoughts that you would prefer to have, the thoughts of your better, more balanced, peaceful, competent self. Often your balancing thoughts will imply an *action plan*—something you can do to remedy the situation or handle it better. Underline any action plans you come up with.

Listed below are alternative responses to the eight limited thinking patterns. It isn't necessary to read through the list from beginning to end. Use it as a reference when you are having problems with a particular pattern.

1. **Filtering.** In order to conquer filtering (i.e., focusing only on negative aspects of a situation), you will have to deliberately shift focus. You can shift focus in two ways: (1) place your attention on coping strategies for dealing with the problem rather than obsessing about the problem itself, or (2) focus on the opposite of your primary mental theme. For example, if you tend to focus on the theme of loss, instead focus on what you still have that is of value. If your theme is danger, focus instead on things in your environment that represent comfort and safety. If your theme is injustice or stupidity or incompetence, shift your focus to what people do that *does* meet with your approval.

2. **Polarized Thinking.** The key to overcoming polarized thinking is to stop making black-or-white judgments. People are not either happy or sad, loving or rejecting, brave or cowardly, smart or stupid. They fall somewhere along a continuum. They are a little bit of each. Human beings are just too complex to be reduced to either/or judgments.

    Instead of making polarized judgments, think in terms of percentages: *About 30 percent of me is scared to death, and 70 percent is holding on and coping;* or *About 60 percent of the time he seems terribly preoccupied with himself, but there's the 40 percent when he can be really generous;* or *Five percent of the time I'm an ignoramus; the rest of the time I do alright.*

3. **Overgeneralization.** Overgeneralization is exaggeration—the tendency to make a mountain out of a molehill. Fight it by *quantifying* instead of using words like "huge," "awful," "massive," "minuscule," and so on. For example, if you catch yourself thinking, *We're buried under massive debt,* rephrase with a quantity: *We owe $47,000.*

    Another way to avoid overgeneralization is to examine how much evidence you really have for your conclusion. If the conclusion is based on one or two cases, a single mistake, or one small symptom, then throw it out until you have more convincing proof. This powerful technique of amassing evidence for and against your automatic negative thoughts is also covered in chapter 8, pertaining to self-blame.

Stop thinking in absolutes by avoiding words such as "every," "all," "always," "none," "never," "everybody," and "nobody." Statements that include these words ignore the exceptions and shades of gray. Replace absolutes with words such as "may," "sometimes," and "often." Be particularly sensitive to absolute predictions about the future, such as "No one will ever love me." They are extremely dangerous because they can become self-fulfilling prophecies.

Pay close attention to the words you use to describe yourself and others. Replace frequently used negative labels with more neutral terms. For example, if you call your habitual caution "cowardice," replace it with "care." Think of your excitable mother as "vivacious" instead of "ditzy." Instead of blaming yourself for being "lazy," call yourself "laid-back."

4. **Mind Reading.** In the long run, you are probably better off making no inferences about people at all. Either believe what they tell you or hold no belief at all until some conclusive evidence comes your way. Treat all of your notions about people as hypotheses to be tested and checked out by asking them.

   Sometimes you can't check out your interpretations. For instance, you may not be ready to ask your daughter if her withdrawal from family life means she's pregnant or taking drugs. But you can allay your anxiety by generating alternative interpretations of her behavior. Perhaps she's in love. Or studying hard. Or depressed about something. Or deeply engrossed in a project. Or worrying about her future. By generating a string of possibilities, you may find a more neutral interpretation that's as likely to be true as your direst suspicions. This process also underlines the fact that you really can't know accurately what others are thinking and feeling unless they tell you.

5. **Catastrophizing.** Catastrophizing is the royal road to anxiety. As soon as you catch yourself catastrophizing, ask yourself, *What are the odds?* Make an honest assessment of the situation in terms of odds or percent of probability. Are the chances of disaster one in 100,000 (.001 percent)? One in a thousand (.1 percent)? One in twenty (5 percent)? Looking at the odds helps you realistically evaluate whatever is frightening you.

6. **Magnifying.** To combat magnifying, stop using words like "terrible," "awful," "disgusting," "horrendous," and so on. In particular, banish phrases like "I can't stand it," "It's impossible," "It's unbearable." You *can* stand it, because history shows that human beings can survive almost any psychological blow and can endure incredible physical pain. You can get used to and cope with almost anything. Try saying to yourself phrases such as *I can cope* and *I can survive this.*

7. **Personalization.** When you catch yourself comparing yourself to others, remind yourself that everyone has strong and weak points. By matching your weak points to others with corresponding strong points, you are just looking for ways to demoralize yourself. The fact is,

human beings are too complex for casual comparisons to have any meaning. It would take you months to catalog and compare all the thousands of traits and abilities of two people. If you assume that others' reactions are often about you, force yourself to check it out. Maybe the reason the boss is frowning isn't that you're late. Make no conclusion unless you are satisfied that you have reasonable evidence and proof.

8. **Shoulds.** Reexamine and question any personal rules or expectations that include the words "should," "ought," or "must." Flexible rules and expectations don't use these words because there are always exceptions and special circumstances. Think of at least three exceptions to your rule, and then imagine all the exceptions there must be that you can't think of. You may get irritated when people don't act according to your values. But your personal values are just that—personal. They may work for you, but, as missionaries have discovered all over the world, they don't always work for others. People aren't all the same. The key is to focus on each person's uniqueness—their particular needs, limitations, fears, and pleasures. Because it is impossible to know all of these complex interrelations, even with intimate partners, you can't be certain whether your values apply to another. You are entitled to an opinion, but allow for the possibility of being wrong. Also, allow for other people to find different things important.

(from McKay, Davis, and Fanning 2021, *Thoughts & Feelings*, 5th ed., 34–35)

Look at the last column to see the balancing and alternative thoughts that Janice came up with. These helped her come up with two action plans, which she underlined.

Situation *When? Where? Who? What happened?*	Feelings *One-word summaries Rate 0–100*	Automatic Thoughts *What you were thinking just before and during the unpleasant feeling*	Limited Thinking Pattern	Balancing or Alternative Thoughts *Underline possible action plans*
Jimmy tore up his book report after we spent an hour on it.	Furious 70 Hopeless 50	Hates me. Does it on purpose to hurt me. He'll never make it in this world.	Personalization Catastrophizing	He's frustrated, can't help it. Don't take it personally. Just hold him tight. He'll find his place in life.
Husband buys three new AC units on credit card.	Angry 85	Fool. He'll ruin us. Homeless. We'll lose the business.	Catastrophizing	He's doing his best. At least they were on sale. We love each other. We're far from homeless.
Made Jimmy cry by pushing him too hard on his math problems.	Ashamed 70	I'm a failure as a mother. I'm blowing it.	Shoulds	I'm doing my best in a hard situation. I don't abuse or neglect him.
Loan officer at the bank kept me waiting, then rushed me, wouldn't let me finish a sentence.	Angry 50 Nervous 75	She can tell I'm desperate. She feels contempt and pity for us. She's supposed to help, not hinder.	Mind Reading Shoulds	She was obviously busy. I admit I was rambling. Next time I'll put it all in writing.

By keeping a Thought Journal, Janice learned how to identify her limited thinking patterns and come up with alternative responses. You will find that using this tool for just a few weeks will help you do the same.

Processes That Increase Flexible Thinking

So far in this chapter you have used classic cognitive behavioral techniques for uncovering, analyzing, and disputing misappraisals. This traditional approach is based on a deficit model that says, "Erroneous automatic thoughts need to be corrected." The flexible thinking skills taught in the rest of the chapter take a more positive psychology approach, based on an expansionist model that says, "Rigid automatic thoughts need to be balanced by more flexible thinking."

Flexible thinking is the ability to analyze a problem, come up with several possible approaches to a solution, evaluate and test the solutions, and put the best solution into action. In this section you will gain more mental flexibility by looking at your automatic thoughts from several new angles.

Flexible Thinking with Negative Predictions

When you habitually use the limited thinking pattern of catastrophizing, you make negative predictions about what will happen to you in the future. There are three exercises you can use to think more flexibly about your negative predictions:

Calculating a Validity Quotient

To find the validity quotient (Allen 2008) for a prediction, ask yourself two questions:

* How many times have you made this prediction in the past five years?

* How many times in the past five years has it come true?

The validity quotient is the number of predictions that come true, divided by the total number of predictions.

Example. June kept having anxious thoughts that her boyfriend would leave her. In the past five years, she estimated worrying about rejection about 100 times. During the same time period, June herself left several relationships, and one ended by mutual agreement. Her validity quotient was 0 divided by 100, which equals zero. Her worries about rejection were totally invalid.

You can also expand the validity quotient to assess the accuracy of predictions in general. How many negative predictions of all types have you made in the past year? How many turned into realities? June used this analysis to recognize that her thoughts predicting rejection of all types, while feeling very certain at the time, were just ideas—not reality. They were not certain to happen; in fact, they had never happened.

Using a Predictions Log

You've looked at the accuracy of past predictions. Now it's time to track the accuracy of predictions as they occur. Every time you seriously start to worry about something, where you imagine a bad or painful outcome, make an entry into a small notebook. Record exactly what you fear will happen, and when. Leave room to write later what actually occurred. Periodically check your Predictions Log to bring it up to date. Did the predicted catastrophe happen or not? Over time, write the actual outcomes under each prediction. The Prediction Log will loosen the certainty that many worries seem to generate. With these thoughts seeming less absolute, they will also trigger less fear.

Example. Annie kept a Predictions Log focused primarily on her fears about her six-year-old daughter. Annie wrote down worst-case predictions about medical problems, relationships with other children, and learning and behavior problems. In the space of three months, Annie logged more than two dozen negative predictions. Yet only one of them ever came true—a lice infestation during a classroom epidemic. As a result of keeping her log, Annie began to take her worries a little less seriously. They more resembled a chance or possibility, rather than a likely outcome. Annie's worries felt softer, less serious, and less scary.

Finding the Purpose of Your Predictions

Every behavior—physical and mental—has a purpose, including your negative predictions. Look back at some of the predictions noted in your Thought Journal or recall some negative predictions you made over the past few weeks. These thoughts are all trying to do one thing—reduce uncertainty. They are seeking to prepare you for bad things that might happen and somehow keep you safe.

But is this working? Think back and notice what happens with your negative predictions. Do you feel more secure, more prepared for danger? Or are you simply more scared? For most people negative predictions leave them feeling more anxious than safe. In fact, the amount of anxiety is often proportionate to the time spent predicting.

When your mind generates scary predictions, ask yourself, *Is this is working?* Is it helping you deal with an uncertain future, or just frightening you more? If the answer is the latter, remind yourself that these are just thoughts, not reality. Name them. Say, *There I go again with the "predictions" or "what ifs" or "future thoughts."* You can notice them, but take them less seriously.

Flexible Thinking About Your Ability to Cope

How would you cope if the worst happened? You may have images of collapse or unmanageable anguish. Your mind may be saying, *I couldn't stand if X happened.* Or your mind might serve up a global sense of catastrophe, and a feeling that you couldn't take it. The best way to deal with these thoughts is the Worst-Case Coping Plan.

Completing a Worst-Case Coping Plan

Make copies of the Coping Plan Worksheet below. Start by assuming that your worst-case prediction has come true. Imagine facing cancer, or a lost job, or the collapse of your relationship. Imagine that you are in the middle of the crisis, trying to grapple with this event you feared. What would you do to cope? Write down your worst-case prediction.

Then, use the following questions to help you complete the "Behavioral Coping" section: How would you cope behaviorally? What specifically would you *do* to face this crisis? If it was a medical problem, what steps would you take to get treatment, negotiate accommodations at work, or secure support at home? If you were facing an end-of-life crisis, how would you deal with financial affairs, the emotional needs of your family, and changes as your physical capacities decline? If it was a financial crisis, outline steps you'd take to reduce expenses, secure a source of funds, or change your living situation. What values would guide your choices in this situation?

Next complete the "Emotional Coping" section. What would you do to deal with the emotional fallout from this crisis? Think about some of the skills you've learned in this book, such as handling emotional outbursts or emotion avoidance. Which of these could be integrated into an emotional coping plan?

Now turn to the "Cognitive Coping" section. Compose some positive thoughts that refute your usual negative self-statements and remind yourself that you are a resilient, capable person.

Finally, move to the "Interpersonal Coping" section. List things you can do with and say to others that will help you cope more effectively.

Coping Plan Worksheet

Worst-Case Prediction: _____

_____

Behavioral Coping:

1. _____
2. _____
3. _____
4. _____
5. _____

Emotional Coping:

1. _____
2. _____
3. _____
4. _____
5. _____

Cognitive Coping:

1. _____
2. _____
3. _____
4. _____
5. _____

Interpersonal Coping: _____

_____

After completing the Coping Plan Worksheet, have your feelings changed in any way regarding the worst-case prediction? Has the fear level gone up or down? Does this prediction seem less overwhelming or less scary to think about?

Example. Anthony had an enduring worry that his marriage was in trouble. He and his wife were in couples therapy, but the sessions only seemed to stir up more conflict. Here is Anthony's Coping Plan Worksheet.

Anthony's Coping Plan Worksheet

Worst-Case Prediction: She calls it quits, says she's got a lawyer and is getting a divorce.

Behavioral Coping:

1.   Get my own lawyer.

2.   Try to explain things to Jeanie (daughter) so she isn't scared.

3.   Work out temporary custody schedule.

4.   Look for a two-bedroom apartment (so Jeanie can have a room).

Emotional Coping:

1.   Radical acceptance meditation.

2.   Spend some time in a beautiful place—Yosemite?

3.   Get support from friends.

4.   Do fun things with Jeanie.

5.   Get back into photography.

Cognitive Coping:

1.   Remember I have a plan.

2.   Try to find positives in my new life.

3.   Try to accept that we're different people with different needs—and that we've been growing apart for a number of years.

Interpersonal Coping: Turn my anger into assertive requests regarding assets and time with Jeanie.

Anthony was surprised, after completing the worksheet, to feel less anxious. He still wanted to keep his marriage, but the coping plan reduced panic and overwhelm when he thought about it ending.

Reviewing Your Coping History

Sometimes it helps to remember that you've faced and coped with crises in the past. On a piece of paper, list five major challenges in the past where you coped more effectively than expected. Now, for each crisis, note the specific ways you coped. Did you do anything that surprised you, or seemed different from your usual response to challenges? Are there common threads across these crises in terms of effective ways you responded?

Example. Rena, when she examined her five successful challenges, noticed that a common thread was assertively asking for what she wanted. She didn't let people push her around, as she often did in other situations. It was illuminating for Rena to see that she did actually possess effective coping skills—she just had to use them.

Flexible Thinking with Focusing on the Negative

When you filter out all the good things in your life and focus on the negative, that is a sure recipe for maintaining depression. Yet you can overcome it with three specific flexible thinking skills.

Developing Big Picture Awareness

Focusing on the negative is like eating dinner and only noticing the food you don't like. As for the rest of the meal—what you might have enjoyed—you simply don't pay attention. Negative focus shows up in countless ways. Whether you're thinking about a vacation, a conversation, a movie, a relationship, a job, a place you lived, or how you're going to spend tomorrow, focusing on the negative turns it into something dark and sad. You simply fail to remember or anticipate anything that feels good.

Developing *big picture awareness* is a way to overcome this cognitive habit. And it's simple to do. After you've said or noticed what you don't like about an experience, add some balancing realities. Acknowledge two things that you liked or appreciated. Make it a rule—you can't think or talk about the negative without identifying two positive aspects.

When looking for the positive, consider these categories:

- Physical pleasure/comfort

- Positive emotion

- Rest/relaxation/relief/peace

- Sense of satisfaction/accomplishment/validation

- Something interesting/exciting/fun

- Learning something

- Feeling of connection/closeness

- Feeling of being loved/appreciated

- Something that feels meaningful/valued

- The feeling of giving something

Put these ten categories on an index card and keep them with you. Then, when you think or speak negatively about something, use these categories to find two aspects that offer a positive balance.

Example. Leah hated visiting her mother-in-law. After complaining to her husband about the last visit, she decided to try big picture awareness. Leah was surprised, when she looked at the list of positive categories, that several applied: (1) her mother-in-law served delicious pastries, (2) Leah had fun playing with her in-laws' collie, and (3) she enjoyed talking about a TV program they both liked.

Big picture awareness requires recognizing that things aren't all good or all bad. Most experiences have multiple components—some feel good, and some don't. Seeing each event as an amalgam of the pleasant and unpleasant, and recognizing both, develops more balanced and flexible thinking.

Seeing Both Sides of the Coin

Embedded in nearly every bad or painful thing that happens is its exact opposite. Most losses include something gained or learned. Moments of failure and weakness often display a paradoxical strength or surprising determination. Right alongside trauma you often see a commitment to survive.

In your life, there have been numerous painful moments, losses, and disappointments. Yet in most of these, if you look, there is something else. The coin has another side. While a negative focus may keep you from turning the situation over to see the positive, it is usually there. You can look past the pain and recognize positive qualities or outcomes that usually accompany even the worst of times.

Try it right now. On a piece of paper, list three serious losses or failures from your past. You're well acquainted with how painful they were, but now flip the coin over. Look for one or more of the following:

- Discovering something learned

- Finding new strength or determination

- Appreciating more the struggles of others

- Having greater acceptance; an ability to let go

- Discovering new or unrecognized parts of yourself

- Finding love and support you didn't know was there

- Gaining more confidence in your ability to cope, face things, and survive

- Experiencing a deeper sense of values, of what matters most

Write down these or other experiences you find on the other side of the coin.

Example. Shana did this exercise looking back at six miserable years in grad school. She'd been extremely depressed and had almost quit numerous times. But the positives, when she sought them, were finding unwavering support from her best friend, gaining a new sense of willpower and perseverance, learning how to take better care of her body, and discovering a commitment to help others in pain.

Finding the Purpose of Negative Focus

All behavior has a function, including thought. Focusing on the negative usually has one of these four functions:

- discharging built-up painful emotions;

- reducing expectations and disappointments;

- avoiding future negative experiences; or

- trying to perfect yourself and get rid of flaws, using negative self-evaluation.

Think about some of the negative thoughts you return to again and again. Which of the above four functions might apply? You may also discover functions for your thoughts that are not listed—that's fine, too.

The key question is are these negative thoughts doing what they're supposed to do? Are they discharging pain, reducing disappointment, helping you avoid future pain, or making you a better person? If not, they aren't working. The fact is that most people get little out of a negative focus. They feel more pain, not less, and more disappointment because they're constantly remembering things that went wrong. Paradoxically, they don't seem able to avoid painful events because that's all they pay attention to. And their self-critical thoughts have the effect of making them feel more flawed, not less.

So when you catch yourself in a negative focus, ask yourself, *Is this working; does this help me in any way?* If the answer is no, acknowledge the thought, label it (*There's one of my "life's no good" thoughts*) and let it go. Of course, it will be back. But just keep labeling and letting it go. Eventually such thoughts will seem less important and less convincing.

Flexible Thinking with Mind Reading and Negative Attributions

Human beings seek to find out why things happen, because if you can explain events, you can often control or anticipate them. The trouble is, the same event or behavior can often be explained different ways. This is particularly true of ambiguous behavior, like someone frowning, shrugging, or moving a little distance away. You can't help trying to interpret such events, even though it's impossible to know for sure what they mean. And if you have a negative bias, you'll often interpret ambiguous behavior as a sign of rejection or displeasure.

The need to explain things is no more evident than when something really bad happens: your job is eliminated, or your child gets sick, or someone you love withdraws. A negative bias here always leaves you at fault. You attribute these events to your own failure, something you did wrong.

The mind grabs onto explanations and often won't let go. Once you have an answer you tend to believe it and stick with it. Cognitive flexibility training helps you be a little less absolute about negative attributions. Instead of clinging with certainty to one explanation, we encourage you to discover multiple explanations for the same event and explore concurrent realities by finding out what other people think. Let's explore both of these processes.

Finding Alternative Explanations

Whenever you answer the question *why* with a negative attribution, such as blaming yourself or someone's negative feeling about you for the event, fill out the Alternative Explanations Worksheet below. Describe the event briefly, along with your negative attribution as to its cause. Then brainstorm five to ten other possible explanations. For example, someone frowning could mean that the person was tired, bored, thinking of something to say, having an unpleasant memory, noticing a physical pain, wanting to go home, worrying about something, and so on. If it seems helpful, you can rate the probability of each alternative on a 3-point scale: 1 = possible; 2 = somewhat likely; 3 = likely.

Alternative Explanations Worksheet

Event:

Attribution:

Alternative Explanations:	Probability:
1.	
2.	
3.	
4.	
5.	
6.	
7.	
8.	
9.	
10.	

It's important to develop alternative explanations *every time you have a negative attribution* because it helps the attribution seem a little less absolute. Once you're a bit less convinced of an attribution, your thinking becomes more flexible and you can see the same event from a number of vantage points.

Example. Let's look at Sam's Alternative Explanations Worksheet to see how this works.

Event: They've asked me to identify four smaller accounts I can give to another sales rep.

Attribution: They think I'm slipping, not doing a good job.

Alternative Explanations:	Probability:
1. New junior reps need some established accounts to get started	2
2. I'm spread thin over too many smaller accounts; need to focus on the big boys	2
3. They're getting me ready for a manager job	1
4. My sales slipped a little, it's a wakeup call	3
5. Everyone's sales slipped this year; they're trying to get the more effective reps to only handle the more productive accounts	3

Sam actually had more alternative explanations than the five we've listed, but you get the idea. He was able to expand his thinking and feel less wedded to the original attribution.

Exploring Concurrent Realities

Sometimes it's helpful to find out what other people think. Maybe they see the same event through a very different lens. When you find yourself seriously caught in a negative attribution, find other people who've witnessed the same event. Ask them what they made of the ambiguous frown, the layoff, the strange remark, or a sudden withdrawal. If you can't find someone who actually witnessed the event, pick a sympathetic friend, describe what happened, and ask your friend for their explanation. Sometimes you might even consider asking the person whose behavior concerns you. Once you've gathered one or two opinions from others, add them to your Alternative Explanations Worksheet and rate their probability.

When Sam told another sales rep about having his accounts reassigned, he was surprised to learn that the rep had experienced the same thing. The rep thought it was because the small accounts were taking too much time and not earning much. Perhaps the company didn't want to service them anymore. Sam added this to his explanations list.

Flexible Thinking with Shoulds

It's important to have values—guiding principles that help you live a life that matters. But values must always be understood in context. The value of being open and truthful may have to play second fiddle to the value of being loving when truthfulness would do unnecessary damage in a particular situation. So values are always acted upon flexibly, depending upon the needs and circumstances of everyone involved.

Rules and shoulds are something different. Shoulds insist that you and others always act a certain way, no matter what. Rules aren't flexible. Rule-bound behavior can get you in trouble because it often brings you into conflict with another person's rules or needs. Since rules and shoulds tend to be absolute—applicable to everyone at all times—we often label ourselves or others as bad or wrong when rules are broken. This results in a lot of anger, guilt, shame, and depression—pain that would be much milder if rules and shoulds were more flexible. To soften shoulds and increase cognitive flexibility, express shoulds as preferences—not absolute rules—by using the word "prefer" rather than "should," "ought," or "must." For example:

- "You should work harder" becomes "I would prefer that you work harder."

- "I should never show fear" becomes "I would prefer not to show fear."

- "I must look confident" becomes "I would prefer to look confident."

- "You should never be late" becomes "I'd prefer you not be late."

Notice that "prefer" softens the absolute quality of shoulds and transforms rules into a personal desire. Start the habit right now. Notice every time the word *should* pops up in your vocabulary and immediate restate the sentence as a preference.

Flexible Thinking Skills You Already Have

Another way to increase your flexible thinking is to identify and build on strengths you already possess. In what areas of your life does your thinking work well for you? Are you a good problem solver at work or school? Can you strategize well on the baseball diamond or basketball court? Are you good at crossword puzzles or Sudoku? Do you have a flair for remembering historical events or movie plots? Can you fix things or cook without a recipe? Are you a loyal and supportive friend to others?

Keep a Flexible Thoughts Record that shows your successful solutions to problem situations. List situations that start out badly but end well thanks to your flexible thinking. Remember times from your past when you coped well with a challenging problem. Use the chart below to describe the problem situation, your feelings, flexible thoughts, solutions, and positive results.

Flexible Thoughts Record

Problem Situation	Feelings	Flexible Thoughts	Solutions	Positive Results

Example. Jack was a bartender, guitar player, and part time DJ who was depressed about his money problems, lack of success, and separation from his wife and daughter, Jenny. It took him weeks to get around to doing this exercise, but then he was surprised at how much it helped him. Here are some of his entries:

Problem Situation	Feelings	Flexible Thoughts	Solutions	Positive Results
Bar is busy, I'm shorthanded, rowdy drunk yelling	Angry, irritated	How can I turn this around? Who can help me?	Defuse situation with humor, get drunk's friends to quiet him	Bar mellows out, drunk leaves, I get good tips
Thanksgiving dinner at mother-in-law's, Wife is upset about meal being late, Jenny cranky	Nervous	If I can cheer up Jenny, her mom will follow. What does she like?	Start playing guitar, singing Jenny's favorite funny song	Jenny sings along, wife laughs, mood lightens
DJ-ing at community fundraiser, rainy night, poor attendance	Depressed, nervous	Use the music to take them from where they are to where I want them.	Spin slow rain song, faster rain song, slow dance, faster dance. Keep my voice bouncy happy	People start dancing. It's not a bad party after all.

In what situations are you able to think more flexibly and clearly? How might you apply your flexible thinking skills to other, less successful areas of your life?

Completing the Flexible Thought Record helped Jack see that he functioned well in small groups of people who were unhappy or conflicted. He was actually pretty good at moving beyond his own negative thoughts and feelings and figuring out what he could do to improve the situation for himself and others. He had a kind of emotional intuition, humor, and contagious energy that others respond to.

Another thing he noticed about his behavior in small groups was his persistence. He was able to stick to his job, his role, or his plan despite social turmoil around him. He realized that he could apply his small group skills and persistence to his stalled career. He joined a "Get Out of Debt" support group. He started looking for a partner with business skills who might join him in opening a night club.

In addition to recognizing and building on your strengths, a final way to broaden your success is to pick something you love to do and do more of that. It can be a simple as making more time to enjoy a favorite but neglected pastime, or delving deeper into a hobby you enjoy. You can take a class or workshop, watch online tutorials, get a how-to book, join a club, travel, order new supplies or art materials, participate in a scientific study, become a volunteer, and so on. Whatever it takes to go further into something you enjoy and are good at.

Jack spent more time listening to music new and old. He practiced guitar more. He spent more time with friends who played music. As his depression lifted, he even got along better with his wife and got to see Jenny more often.

Where will your flexible thinking skills take you?

Summary

In this chapter you have learned to identify, refute, and revise your cognitive misappraisals and replace them with more positive, flexible thinking. Using these tools regularly will significantly lessen your emotional pain and enable you to view yourself, others, and life, through a more positive lens.

From here, return to the assessment chapter and look at your next highest scores on the Comprehensive Coping Inventory–55. That will tell you which chapter to work on next.

CHAPTER 8

Self-Esteem: From Self-Blame to Self-Compassion

Your high score on section 8 of the Comprehensive Coping Inventory–55 indicates that you tend to blame yourself for whatever distress you feel, and consequently have low self-esteem. Self-esteem means that you like, accept, and feel kindly toward yourself. It means that you acknowledge yourself as a fallible human being, prone to making mistakes from time to time, especially when you are under stress. Self-esteem assures you that you are doing your best at any given moment to live according to your values and treat others as you would like to be treated yourself. In contrast, when you have low self-esteem, you constantly blame yourself for your faults and failings rather than feel compassion for yourself.

Self-blame can arise for many reasons: your genetic makeup, your early family history, or some later traumatic experiences. Whatever its origin, self-blame can be reduced and self-compassion can be developed using the change processes in this chapter. First you'll learn the function of self-blame thoughts and why they persist. Then you'll have a chance to experience powerful exercises in uncovering and countering your self-blame thoughts. Finally, you'll learn how to develop compassion for yourself through experiencing compassion for others.

Self-Blame: What It Is

The definition of self-blame is rather self-evident: a pattern of blaming yourself for what goes wrong in your life. But what is the function of self-blaming thoughts?

I'm blowing this…I sound stupid…It's all my fault…Foolish…Loser…Screwing up…I'll never learn… Serves me right…

These are painful judgments and criticisms to apply to anyone, much less yourself. They really hurt. If these kinds of self-blaming thoughts are so painful, why don't you just stop having them? Why do these self-blaming thoughts persist?

There must be some benefit or payoff to self-blaming thoughts, or people would not repeat them day after day, year after year. Self-blaming thoughts persist because they have one or all of these three functions:

1. To avoid sadness, disappointment, and a sense of loss when things don't go well. You cover up these negative feelings with anger at yourself.

2. To create the illusion of control. If you judge and attack yourself enough, you'll stop making mistakes and things will go well in your life.

3. To punish yourself. Somehow you feel you deserve to be punished when things go wrong, and so you punish yourself.

Fortunately, it's possible to curtail your pattern of self-blame, which we'll cover next.

Processes That Reduce Self-Blame

In short, reducing self-blame boils down to counting, questioning, and weighing evidence for your self-blaming thoughts. We'll walk you through these exercises below.

Counting Self-Blame Thoughts

The first step in reducing the frequency of self-blame thoughts is to keep track of the thoughts you have and how often you have them. For about a week, keep this Counting Self-Blame Thoughts record.

Counting Self-Blame Thoughts

Situations When? Where? Who? What happened?	Feelings One-word summaries, rated 0–100	Self-Blame Thoughts What you were thinking just before and during the unpleasant feeling	Occurrences Make a mark each time you have this thought.

Example. Audrey, twenty-two years old, had dropped out of college and was working part time at her boyfriend Paul's auto shop. Paul was abusive toward her, and she was worrying about whether to tell him she was pregnant. Here are some of Audrey's journal entries:

Situations When? Where? Who? What happened?	Feelings One-word summaries, rated 0–100	Self-Blame Thoughts What you were thinking just before and during the unpleasant feeling	Occurrences Make a mark each time you have this thought.
At work, Paul criticizes me	Ashamed 65 worthless 70	I can't do anything right	X X X X X
Morning sickness, smelling foods, nauseated during day	Hopeless 90 Scared 85	I should tell him I'm pregnant, he'll leave me, I'm so stupid	X X X X
Helping Joan plan her graduation party	Jealous 40	She's on her way, I'm a loser	X X X

Questioning Self-Blame Thoughts

For each of your recurring self-blame thoughts, ask these three questions:

1. **How old is this self-blame thought?** Think back as far as you can to the first times you had this thought.

   When Audrey asked herself how old her self-blaming thoughts were, she realized that they did not have much to do with her current boyfriend or even her pregnancy. From childhood she had felt worthless whenever her mom or her teachers criticized her, and she blamed herself for being incompetent.

2. **What's this thought in the service of?** Figure out the purpose of the thought. It might be to avoid something, to protect yourself from something, or to punish yourself for something.

   In Audrey's case, she realized that her self-blaming thoughts were a way of punishing herself for her mistakes and a way of encouraging herself to do better.

3. **How has this thought worked for me?** Examine how well this thought has worked in protecting you, avoiding certain situations, or punishing yourself.

Audrey's self-blaming thoughts had never worked for her. Instead of motivating her to try harder, they discouraged and immobilized her.

Weighing Evidence for Your Self-Blame Thoughts

Another process for working on your automatic thoughts is to weigh the evidence for and against the thoughts. In the worksheet below, list some old and more recent situations, feelings, and self-blame thoughts from your Counting Self-Blame Thoughts record. This time, write the evidence for each thought in the fourth column. In what ways does this thought make sense in the situation? What is its justification or reason for occurring?

In the fifth column, write all the evidence against each thought. How does each thought not make sense?

How does it conflict with the reality of the situation, with what you know to be true about yourself and others?

In the sixth column, write balancing or alternative thoughts, ones for which you have strong evidence, ones that make more sense in the situation. Underline any of your balancing and alternative thoughts that suggest an action plan, something you can follow through with in your life.

In the last column, re-rate your feelings and notice if their intensity has lessened.

Weighing Evidence for Your Self-Blame Thoughts

Situation When? Where? Who? What happened?	Feelings One-word summaries Rated 0–100	Self-Blame Thoughts What you were thinking just before and during the unpleasant feeling	Evidence For	Evidence Against	Balancing or Alternative Thoughts Underline possible action plans.	Re-rate Feelings 0–100

Example. Felicia ran a small boutique that was in financial trouble. Her son Jimmy had dyslexia and hyperactivity and has trouble in school. Weighing the evidence was Felicia's favorite exercise for dealing with her self-blame thoughts. She was on the high school debate team, and she remembered liking the process of breaking a resolution down into the evidence supporting it and the evidence refuting it. Here are some of her many entries:

Situation When? Where? Who? What happened?	Feelings One-word summaries Rated 0–100	Self-Blame Thoughts What you were thinking just before and during the unpleasant feeling	Evidence For	Evidence Against	Balancing or Alternative Thoughts Underline possible action plans.	Re-rate Feelings 0–100
Applying for a loan at the bank. Loan officer frowning.	Angry 50 Nervous 75	She can tell I'm desperate, don't deserve the loan. I wouldn't loan money to me either.	She didn't make eye contact, wouldn't let me finish a sentence, kept looking over at the lady at the front desk.	She gave me the correct forms and told me how to fill them out. Smiled at me once, said "Sorry we're so busy."	I have no way of knowing what her thoughts are. Stop mind reading. Concentrate on filling out the application. Wait and see.	
Guidance counselor called and asked to meet about Jimmy's schoolwork	Afraid 85 Guilty 70	It's my fault, I should have helped him more. He's failing in school like I did.	His grades have gotten worse, he's still disruptive in class.	He did well on the art project, did extra work at home. In many ways he's different than I was in school.	We're both doing our best. Bring in the art project to show her.	
Husband says we should hire a tutor for Jimmy	Angry 60 Guilty 60	I'm incompetent as a mother. It's my fault. Can't afford it.	He acts nervous when he says this, looks away. The bank statement, the bills.	Husband said I'm a big help to Jimmy but don't have time. Husband said maybe his grandma can help.	This is his way of helping, solving the problem. Hear him out, call grandma, don't take things so personally.	

(Adapted from McKay, Davis, and Fanning 2021, *Thoughts & Feelings*, 5th ed.)

Like Felicia, you will likely find that this exercise helps you significantly reduce your self-blaming tendencies, opening the door for greater self-compassion.

Processes That Increase Self-Compassion

The Dalai Lama's definition of compassion is "sensitivity to suffering with motivation to alleviate or prevent it." There are two distinct parts to his view: the capacity to observe painful emotions without pushing them away or being overwhelmed, and the desire to alleviate and prevent suffering.

Compassion for others and compassion for yourself are two sides of the same coin. It's not easy to open yourself to your own pain and the pain of others without judgment. It's harder to actively feel empathy for yourself and others than to passively send your "hopes and prayers." The processes described in this section will help you develop these skills.

Compassion Record

Carry a card or sheet of paper with you every day for a week. Label one side "Others" and use it to note every act of kindness, support, or love directed toward you. Record each time someone asks how you are, compliments you, smiles at you, gives you something, helps you in some way, notices how you're feeling, and so on. Make it your daily intention not only to notice these small acts of kindness, but to appreciate them with feelings of gratitude.

Label the other side of your card or paper "Me." There you will make a note every time you do something kind, supportive, or loving for someone else or for yourself. Keep track of the times you notice how someone else is feeling, do a favor for someone, or give a compliment. Also note when you do something just for yourself, have a kind thought about yourself, or notice how you are feeling with compassion and a lack of judgment.

After a few days, see how you are doing. If you are like most self-blamers, you will have ample entries on the "Others" side of your journal, quite a few examples on the "Me" side of compassion toward other people, but fewer instances where you felt or expressed compassion for yourself. If this is true for you, you need to put self-compassion into action. For the for the rest of the week and the following week, once each day:

- Do something that you wouldn't usually do, something that constitutes a special treat for you. You might listen to music with your eyes closed, doing nothing else. Or take a walk around the block. Maybe slowly rub hand lotion all over your arms and hands. Sit somewhere quiet and have a cup of tea or fresh fruit juice. Visit a store or gallery and enjoy gazing at beautiful things.

- Don't pick things that you tend to overindulge in anyway, like drinking, using drugs, watching online porn, or shopping.

- Tell yourself, *This is a special moment, just for me. This treat is good for me and I deserve it. I am expressing toward myself the compassion and loving-kindness that I wish for all people.*

- Note your self-compassionate action on the "Me" side of your paper for that day.

Example. When Jackson started his compassion journal, he found, on the "Others" side, that he discounted the nice things others did for him and said to him. Keeping the journal helped him notice that compassion was in the air all around him, but he was tone deaf to it much of the time. On the "Me" side of things, he managed to treat others with compassion a few times. Keeping the journal reminded him to pay better attention to the feelings and situations of others and express more appreciation to them.

Jackson's "Me" side of the journal had very few self-compassionate experiences, so he started doing at least one special thing for himself each to put in his compassion journal. One day he took the time to enjoy taking a bath instead of his usual quick shower. He relaxed in the tub and listened to some favorite old punk songs on his phone. Other days he did the self-compassionate body scan exercise that follows. Gradually he developed the ability to temper his self-blame with genuine self-compassion.

Self-Compassionate Body Scan

This is a good exercise to develop compassion for your physical self.

Find a time when you will not be disturbed, and lie down on your back in a comfortable spot, with the intention of feeling compassion for yourself. Cover yourself with a blanket if you wish, uncross your arms and legs, and close your eyes.

Breathe in and out slowly, focusing on the rise and fall of your chest and stomach. Gradually scan your whole body. Scan from your feet to your ankles, your calves, slowly all the way up to your head. Notice any sensations on your skin, where the weight of gravity is pressing down, points of contact with the surface you're lying on. Whatever you feel—comfort, discomfort, or neither—accept it with loving-kindness toward your body.

You are not trying to make anything happen or fix anything, just noticing and accepting what is going on in your body. Put your hand on your heart and imagine that with each inhalation you are breathing in a warm glow of kindness. Imagine that with every exhalation you are breathing out any tension or negative, self-blaming thoughts.

You may get so relaxed that you fall asleep. That's fine. Allow yourself to enjoy the nap. You definitely will get distracted. That's fine too. Just refocus on your breathing, keeping a tender regard toward yourself, with no blame for getting it wrong.

When you are ready to end this session, thank your body for how it supports you and keeps you going from day to day. Open your eyes, reorient to your surroundings, and get up refreshed.

Compassion for the Vulnerable Self

In this exercise you will adopt the persona of a kind, wise, strong person. From that point of view you will observe yourself in a difficult situation from your past, feeling compassion toward yourself and a desire to help.

Sit upright in a comfortable chair. Close your eyes and focus on slow breathing, in and out, for a few moments.

Allow sensations of calm, warmth, and strength to fill your body. Let a kind smile cross your lips. Imagine being filled with a deeply felt sense of kindness and a committed desire to help yourself and all those who are suffering. Feel this kind commitment growing in you.

Imagine that with this kind motivation you are filled with a deep wisdom and understanding. You are able to think flexibly, see things from multiple perspectives, and figure out what to do in any situation.

Imagine that alongside this wisdom, you have a powerful feeling of confidence and courage. You know that whatever happens, you can work with it. You know that you can offer real help to yourself and others.

Bring to mind a situation you've struggled with recently, one in which you were really anxious, afraid, or self-critical. Imagine that you are watching yourself struggle in this stressful time. See and hear everything that went on, what you and others did, but experience the scene from the outside, as a wise, strong, deeply compassionate observer.

From this kind, wise, confident perspective, allow yourself to be touched by your suffering and to have compassion for this vulnerable version of yourself in the past. Notice how in the stress and struggle of the moment, you were doing your best to cope. Realize that it makes total sense that you would have been scared or depressed or angry, that you might have lashed out or retreated, might have acted in self-destructive or self-defeating ways.

Imagine that this strong, compassionate version of you could be there in the past with the vulnerable you. Imagine you're there with yourself and you can see and hear each other. Consider how you would be there for your vulnerable self. You know yourself better than anyone else, what you need and how you feel. How would you help your vulnerable self?

Imagine your compassionate self sitting there with your vulnerable self, sending kindness, understanding, and support. You understand what you're going through and how hard it is.

Allow yourself to feel good about supporting your vulnerable self and imagine being filled with the kindness, support, and encouragement you're sending out.

From this compassionate perspective, what would you want your vulnerable self to understand?

When you are ready, remind yourself of your surroundings and open your eyes.

(adapted from Kolts 2016, *CFT Made Simple: A Clinician's Guide to Practicing Compassion-Focused Therapy*)

A similar exercise, called Tonglen meditation, is a traditional Tibetan Buddhist technique that is also well suited for fostering self-compassion. Instead of showing compassion to your vulnerable self from the past, as in the previous exercise, Tonglen meditation allows you to offer compassion to your current, ordinary self who is suffering. You can find the exercise on the website for this book, at http://www.newharbinger.com/50218.

Compassionate Letter Writing

If the more meditative exercises don't appeal to you, this one is a good alternative. You'll produce a love letter to yourself that you can reread when you are under stress and you slip back into self-blame.

- Pretend that you are your own best friend, a steadfast blood brother or sister who is always there for you, who supports you—no matter what—with unconditional love. From the point of view of that persona, use the form below to write yourself a letter.

- Start with your name. It can be your real, regular name, a nickname, or some special name that you wish a friend would call you, like "Darling" or "Dearest."

- In the next space, briefly describe a typical stressful situation in which you tend to blame yourself.

- The nest space is for the feelings you typically have in this situation.

- The "However" space is the most important part, where you imagine how your very best friend would express their love, acceptance, and support for you. Write from the vantage point of a person who has nothing but true compassion for you, who feels your depression or anger or fear with you, who knows how dark it can get in your world, who understands and forgives everything, and who loves and supports you no matter what.

- If the format of filling in blanks seems awkward for you, write a letter in your own format. Just be sure to include the key components: your triggers; feelings; self-blaming thoughts; and the statements of love, acceptance, and support.

Dear (Your name) _____:

I know that when (your stressful situation happens) _____
_____

you feel (emotions) _____.

And you blame yourself this way: _____

However, _____
_____
_____
_____
_____

Love,

Your Friend Forever

If you want, you can add another section of this letter, or as many as you like, describing a different stressful situation that evoke self-blame. When your letter is done, put it away for a few hours or until tomorrow, and then reread it. Really take in the words and their meaning as if you were reading them for the first time. Absorb the underlying message that regardless of your past, your limitations, or your choices, you are worthy of love and respect.

Example. Luanne was a clerk at the Department of Motor Vehicles, a single mother of a daughter with severe allergies and dyslexia, and an occasional binge drinker. This is how she wrote her letter:

Dear Luanne _____:

I know that when Mr. Sanchez at work yells at you about a mistake or how slow you are, you feel <u>depressed.</u>

And you blame yourself this way: <u>I'm stupid, useless.</u>

However, <u>I also know that you are doing your best in a hard, complicated job, with customers who are stressed out and don't understand the system. I appreciate how you keep showing up on the job.</u>

AND

I know that when <u>Bunny's school calls about her low grades, distractions, and absences,</u>

you feel <u>sad and guilty.</u>

And you blame yourself this way: <u>It's my fault. I'm failing her.</u>

However, <u>you have honestly tried many things to help your daughter with her schoolwork. You and she have been dealt a hard hand in life, dealing with serious challenges. No matter what the outcome with Bunny's school is, I love and support you. I will be there for you.</u>

AND

I know that when <u>it seems like everything is weighing down on you and you will be crushed,</u>

you feel <u>devastated.</u>

And you blame yourself this way: <u>I'm broken, there's something wrong with me. I need a drink to dull the pain.</u>

However, <u>I believe that at any given moment, you are doing what seems best, and sometimes you have needed to zone out for a while. You realize that calling in sick and drinking is not really in line with your values for you or Bunny, and you are working hard to do things differently. Just know this: You can't do anything so bad that it would make me love you less. I will always be there for you.</u>

Love,

Your Forever Friend

Compassionate Percentages

Your self-blaming thoughts may feel like they apply one hundred percent, to everything, all the time. But that's not the case. In this self-compassion exercise you systematically break down the percentages. Start by completing these four sentences:

A negative trait that I blame myself for is _____.

I display this trait _____ percent of the time.

I display this trait especially in these domains _____

_____.

(family, relationship, parenting, friends, work, education/
training, recreation, spirituality, citizenship, physical care)

I have this trait because of these influences in my background _____

_____.

Now consider these three questions:

- When you are not displaying this negative trait, are you the same person?

- Outside of the triggering domains, when you are not displaying this negative trait, who are you then?

- Considering your genes, you early family history, and the unavoidable traumas of life, are you entirely to blame for this negative trait?

Having considered these questions, write a more compassionate self-description that takes the percentages into account:

_____

_____

_____

_____

Example. Here is how Jean completed this exercise:

A negative trait that I blame myself for is <u>shyness and withdrawing from people.</u>

I display this trait _____<u>35</u>_____ percent of the time.

I display this trait especially in these domains: <u>with potential friends, with work colleagues, and with</u> <u>teachers.</u>

I have this trait because of these influences in my background: <u>a critical mother, absent father, super</u> <u>successful brother, bad breakup with Larry.</u>

A more compassionate self-description would be: <u>I am only shy and withdrawn 35 percent of the time,</u> <u>especially with men I don't know, workmates I don't know well, and authority figures like professors. The</u> <u>majority of the time I am not shy, especially with my old friends and my sister Kat. This all makes sense</u> <u>given my introverted personality, my upbringing, and how Larry dumped me.</u>

Compose Your Own Self-Compassion Mantra

For centuries, healers, gurus, spiritual advisors, psychologists, ministers, coaches, and motivational speakers have been touting the advantages of repeating short positive statements to yourself. Call them what you will—mantras, slogans, pep talks, affirmations, prayers, mottoes, or mission statements—these short sayings are powerful.

Kristin Neff (2011) gives her own self-compassion mantra as an example: *This is a moment of suffering. Suffering is part of life. May I be kind to myself in this moment. May I give myself the compassion I need.*

Use this one or come up with your own, and say it to yourself whenever you catch yourself in a self-blaming stance.

Self-Compassion Journal

Once a day for the next seven days, write down the most self-blaming experience you had in the past 24 hours. It can be an actual event you participated in, some information you received, or a purely mental or emotional experience. Include what happened, your thoughts, your feelings, and how you blamed yourself.

Finish with a compassionate response to the experience. Include these three points:

1. As a human being, I am bound to have this kind of experience.

2. I can be mindful of my self-blaming thoughts and let them pass away, as they naturally tend to do.

3. I can practice loving-kindness toward myself.

Self-Compassion Journal

Experience	How I Blamed Myself	Compassionate Response
		As a human being, I am bound to have this kind of experience. I can be mindful of my self-blaming thoughts and let them pass away, as they naturally tend to do. I can practice loving-kindness toward myself.
		As a human being, I am bound to have this kind of experience. I can be mindful of my self-blaming thoughts and let them pass away, as they naturally tend to do. I can practice loving-kindness toward myself.
		As a human being, I am bound to have this kind of experience. I can be mindful of my self-blaming thoughts and let them pass away, as they naturally tend to do. I can practice loving-kindness toward myself.

Experience	How I Blamed Myself	Compassionate Response
		As a human being, I am bound to have this kind of experience. I can be mindful of my self-blaming thoughts and let them pass away, as they naturally tend to do. I can practice loving-kindness toward myself.
		As a human being, I am bound to have this kind of experience. I can be mindful of my self-blaming thoughts and let them pass away, as they naturally tend to do. I can practice loving-kindness toward myself.
		As a human being, I am bound to have this kind of experience. I can be mindful of my self-blaming thoughts and let them pass away, as they naturally tend to do. I can practice loving-kindness toward myself.
		As a human being, I am bound to have this kind of experience. I can be mindful of my self-blaming thoughts and let them pass away, as they naturally tend to do. I can practice loving-kindness toward myself.

Summary

In this chapter you uncovered the many ways you tend to blame yourself. Then you used meditative and written exercises to develop your ability to feel compassion for yourself and others. In doing so, you have found ways to turn self-blame into self-esteem. You can be proud of the work you've done and the results you've enjoyed.

From here, return to the assessment chapter and look at your next highest scores on the Comprehensive Coping Inventory–55. That will tell you which chapter to work on next.

CHAPTER 9

Patience: From Blaming Others to Compassion

You have turned to this chapter because you scored high on section 9 of the Comprehensive Coping Inventory–55, "Blaming Others." The psychological term for this is *externalizing*, a way of coping with painful feelings of shame, fear, embarrassment, loss, or failure. You tend to attribute your pain to the behavior of other people; you experience it as their fault, their error, or their deliberate choice. Externalizing helps you feel blameless for painful experiences; however, the downside of externalizing is chronic anger and a feeling of helplessness.

Your high externalizing score indicates that you struggle with significant levels of anger and dissatisfaction with the behavior of others. Anger takes a toll on your well-being and can result in depression. In this chapter you'll learn proven techniques to turn your tendency to blame others for your pain—externalization—into patience and compassion.

Externalizing: What It Is

Externalizing is a coping mechanism that relieves you of feeling responsible and at fault for your pain. Further, it releases you from any obligation to solve the problem. By blaming others, the fault and responsibility lie with them. You are a victim; you have done no wrong; any feelings of shame and failure are obscured by a sense of righteousness.

Externalizing, or blaming others for your distress, usually triggers anger. Frequent externalizing results in chronic anger. The driver for chronic anger can be understood in a simple formula: pain + blame = externalizing/anger. Pain without blame will *not* trigger anger and all its negative consequences. Blame without pain is just a thought devoid of heat and emotion. So externalizing requires both components. Something has to hurt. And you have *attributed* that pain to the willful, wrong behavior of someone else.

Externalizing can result in three serious outcomes: (1) damaged and lost relationships, (2) chronic physiological arousal that impacts health and elevates the death rate from all causes (Shekelle et al. 1983), and (3) increased helplessness and depression because you experience a lack of control over your pain and problems. The change processes that follow will enable you to avoid these outcomes and live with more compassion.

Processes That Reduce Externalizing

The techniques you'll learn in this chapter are based on two psychological approaches: cognitive and relaxation coping skills (CRCS) and opposite action.

CRCS has been shown through extensive research to be highly effective in relieving chronic anger and the mindset (blaming) at the root of externalizing (Deffenbacher 1988, 1993, 1994; Deffenbacher and McKay 2000). CRCS results in very significant reductions in anger episodes and intensity while also improving relationships and relationship satisfaction (Deffenbacher et al. 1996). By significantly reducing chronic anger and externalizing, CRCS can not only help to improve your relationships and emotional well-being, but, as you've seen above, lessen your risk of related negative physiological outcomes.

Opposite action (Linehan 1993)—increasing kindness and compassion responses—not only reduces anger, but increases the frequency of empathic responses, enabling you to build a new, accepting framework that will profoundly change relationships in every domain of your life. We'll be focusing on opposite action in the last part of the chapter.

Controlling your anger requires four component skills—anger recognition, anger relaxation (release), anger restructuring (changing your anger-triggering thoughts), and nonviolent communication. Let's get started with the first step: noticing your anger and the moment of choice.

Anger Recognition

What are the red flags that say you've been triggered by anger? Think about recent anger episodes. What did you notice as the first indication that you were inflamed? Did you experience any of these signs?

- ☐ a feeling of heat in your body
- ☐ a tightness in your abdomen, arms, or fists
- ☐ an elevated heart or breathing rate
- ☐ a sense of arousal and a drive to attack
- ☐ a sense that you have been a victim and a desire for retribution or payback
- ☐ other _____

Your anger indicators. These markers, whichever you recognize, are signals that you have been conscripted by anger. Check the ones that most conform to what anger feels like to you. Are these the physical and mental experiences that are present when your anger erupts? If you have additional or different anger indicators, write them down on the line for "other."

Recognizing anger before you act is a first and crucial step to anger control. Write your anger indicators on a piece of paper and tape it to your bathroom mirror or some other object you see each day.

Your morning intention and the moment of choice. Review your anger indicators each morning and form an active intention that on this day you'll watch for them *before* expressing anger. Observing your anger—noticing signs of the emotion—can give you space to choose a different response.

Training and committing yourself each day to recognize the anger indicators when they first show up can start to liberate you from emotion-driven behavior. Instead of getting loud and verbally aggressive, you'll have new and more effective options for getting your needs met.

Anger Relaxation

Anger and relaxation don't seem to go together—but they can. Learning to relax at the moment of anger recognition can cool you down so your emotion is less intense, less urgent, and less demanding that you *do* something.

Learning the Techniques

Here are three strategies to help you relax; see which work best for you:

Diaphragmatic breathing. Deep, diaphragmatic breathing relaxes you by stretching and releasing tension in your diaphragm. To learn diaphragmatic breathing, place one hand on your abdomen (just above your belt line) and the other on your upper chest. Take a slow in-breath so only the hand on your abdomen moves—the hand on your chest should not. Just push the air way down to your belly, letting it expand and stretch as you do. As you take each breath, notice your belly rise and fall, and experience a growing sense of calm.

If you have trouble pushing all the air into your belly, or you find the hand on your chest moving, it can be helpful to press on your belly with one hand—then focus your attention on pushing that hand out with your breath.

Practice diaphragmatic breathing three times a day for the next week.

Relaxation without tension. This stress-reduction process helps you systematically relax major muscle groups in your body while taking a diaphragmatic breath and saying a cue word to yourself that triggers muscle release. Here's how it works.

1. Choose a cue word that represents or symbolizes calm. It could be a relaxing color (blue, gold); it might be the name of a peaceful place; it could be a command (relax now, let go); it could be a sound, like *ohm*.

2. Identify the major muscle groups you will relax:

    • forehead, face, jaw, and neck

    • arms and shoulders

    • back

    • abdomen and chest

    • buttocks, legs, and feet

3. Take a breath, say your cue word at the top of the breath, and then release the breath while relaxing away tension in the first muscle group. Just notice any areas of tension in your forehead, face, jaw, and neck, and release them as you slowly let go of the breath. Repeat with a second breath to further relax away tension.

4. Continue the process described above for each of the five muscle groups.

Practice relaxation without tension (with diaphragmatic breathing) three times a day for the next week.

Cue-controlled breathing. The cue word you chose for relaxation without tension can be put to new use. Now you will inhale deeply, note your cue word, and, as you exhale, release tension throughout your entire body. You'll notice at the top of your breath any areas of muscle tightness and, as your breath releases (with your cue word), you can deliberately let go of all tension in your body.

This powerful technique can help you relax deeply in 30 to 60 seconds. Practice ten cue-controlled breaths three times a day (along with diaphragmatic breathing and relaxation without tension).

Practicing Anger Relaxation

After a week's practice with diaphragmatic breathing, relaxation without tension, and cue-controlled breathing, it's time to learn how to relax *when you're angry*. To do this you'll need to identify three anger upsets that have occurred recently. Write down the moments of each scene that most drive your anger. Include the situation and environment, who's there, what is said or done. What do you see and hear? What are your thoughts? What do you feel in your body?

Anger Rehearsal Worksheet

Scene 1:

Scene 2:

Scene 3:

Now visualize Scene 1. Watch the scene as you would a movie and remember your anger-evoking thoughts until you feel actual anger arousal. Note how angry you are on a 1–10 scale. At this point, let go of the scene and begin diaphragmatic breathing. Continue deep breathing until the anger level has reduced 2–3 points on the scale.

Visualize Scene 2 and repeat the process using relaxation without tension. Again, rate your anger after visualizing the scene and after practicing relaxation. Finally, visualize Scene 3 and rate your anger before and after utilizing cue-controlled breathing.

So far so good. But more practice is needed to strengthen your relaxation skills. On your next rehearsal, change it up. Use relaxation without tension on Scene 1, cue-controlled breathing on Scene 2, and diaphragmatic breathing on Scene 3. On the final practice session, switch to cue-controlled breathing on Scene 1, diaphragmatic breathing on Scene 2, and relaxation without tension on Scene 3.

For each rehearsal, use the relaxation response to reduce your anger 2–3 points. This will give you a stronger sense of control and confidence in your relaxation abilities when anger ignites.

Anger Relaxation Worksheet

Instructions: Practice relaxation with each anger scene three times (P-1, P-2, P-3). Rate your anger level after visualizing each scene. Then re-rate your anger after using your relaxation response.

Anger Scene 1: _____

Anger level (1–10) after visualization: Practice 1 _____   Practice 2 _____   Practice 3 _____

P-1: Using diaphragmatic breathing   Anger level (1–10) _____

P-2: Using relaxation without tension   Anger level (1–10) _____

P-3: Using cue-controlled breathing   Anger level (1–10) _____

Anger Scene 2: _____

Anger level (1–10) after visualization: Practice 1 _____   Practice 2 _____   Practice 3 _____

P-1: Using relaxation without tension   Anger level (1–10) _____

P-2: Using cue-controlled breathing   Anger level (1–10) _____

P-3: Using diaphragmatic breathing   Anger level (1–10) _____

Anger Scene 3: _____

Anger level (1–10) after visualization: Practice 1 _____   Practice 2 _____   Practice 3 _____

P-1: Using cue-controlled breathing   Anger level (1–10) _____

P-2: Using diaphragmatic breathing   Anger level (1–10) _____

P-3: Using relaxation without tension   Anger level (1–10) _____

You can practice anger relaxation with additional anger scenes. The more you practice, the more control you will gain over anger-driven behavior.

Putting Anger Relaxation to Work

After the first week of anger relaxation practice, you'll be ready to apply your relaxation skills to real-life anger events. Now, the moment you recognize anger is also the moment of choice. You can quickly relax (with some deep breaths or cue-controlled breaths to relax part or all of your body) or slip into emotion-driven behavior. Try, with each anger event, to practice relaxation before you say or do anything.

Anger Restructuring*—Changing Anger-Triggering Thoughts

There are five types of trigger thoughts that ignite anger. You can't get angry without them, and you'll feel much less angry if you learn to restructure them. The five anger triggers are:

1. **Blaming.** The thought here is that people are doing bad things to you on purpose. They're causing you pain; they're hurting you or doing damage. Examples include:

    *   I could really enjoy this vacation if it weren't for your constant complaining and always finding fault with things.

    *   If you really cared about me, you would have helped me with the resume, and then I would have gotten that job.

    *   You always ask me to give you a ride and then take all day to get dressed so I'll be late for my meeting.

2. **Inflammatory global labeling.** These thoughts are sweeping, negative judgments about people whose behavior you don't like. But instead of focusing on the behavior, the label characterizes the *person* as being totally wrong, bad, and worthless. These judgments are often delivered as one-word epithets. Examples include:

    *   My girlfriend is a total bitch.

    *   That driver who just cut me off is a complete a-hole.

    *   What a jerk. He doesn't know anything.

    *   That bastard deserves to be beaten with a stick for what he did.

---

*   Anger restructuring process adapted from *The Anger Control Workbook* by M. McKay and P. D. Rogers, 2000

3. **Misattributions.** These thoughts are a form of mind-reading—jumping to conclusions about the motives for another person's behavior. The person does something that annoys you, and you *assume* the "real" reason. You focus on a single explanation: they were deliberately trying to be mean to you, they were selfishly causing you upset. Examples include:

    - He acted like he just wanted to correct my grammar, but he was really trying to make me look stupid.

    - I know she was just doing that to embarrass me in front of everyone.

    - What a dumb argument. He's really out to get me.

    - The only reason she's late is to piss me off.

4. **Overgeneralization.** These thoughts make any problem look bigger by using words such as "never," "always," "nobody," "everybody," "all the time," and so on. Such thoughts make an occasional event feel like something intolerable and ongoing. By exaggerating with overgeneralizations, you tend to jack up your angry response. Examples include:

    - She's always doing things like that to make me look bad.

    - Nobody seems to know what they're doing around here.

    - You're never ready on time, so we're always late for everything.

    - Everybody is always asking me to do them a favor.

5. **Demanding/commanding.** These thoughts turn your personal preferences into absolute rules for living. Words such as "should," "got to," "have to," and "ought to" create moral dictates. When others ignore your rules, it seems to justify anger and verbal punishment. Examples include:

    - They shouldn't have done that—it was absolutely wrong.

    - He isn't being fair. He should listen to me.

    - She ought to know better. That was bound to fail.

    - This is the way it's got to be. Any other way is just plain stupid.

Developing Trigger-Thought Countermeasures

The goal now is to develop two or three effective coping thoughts to deal with anger triggers so they won't be so inflaming. The following countermeasures (rules) will help you restructure the five types of anger triggers:

Blaming. (1) Make a coping plan to solve the problem yourself. (2) Recognize that people are mostly doing the best they can—what they think will best meet their needs.

Misattributions. (1) Check out your assumptions about other people's motives. (2) Find alternative explanations for the problem behavior.

Inflammatory global labeling. (1) Be specific: focus on behavior, not the person as a whole.

Overgeneralization. (1) Avoid general terms like "always," "all," and "every." (2) Use specific and accurate descriptions. (3) Look for exceptions to the rule. Recall how people sometimes act contrary to their tendencies.

Demanding/commanding. (1) Remind yourself that people rarely do what they should do, only what they need or want to do. (2) Stay with your wants, desires, and preferences—not should. Think, "I'd prefer," not "You ought to."

Using General Coping Thoughts

In addition to the countermeasures above, use any of these general coping thoughts to calm anger at the moment of choice when you first recognize you're upset.

General Coping Thoughts List

Take a deep breath and relax.

Getting upset won't help.

As long as I keep my cool, I'm in control.

Easy does it—there's nothing to be gained in getting mad.

I'm not going to let them get to me.

I can't change them with anger; I'll just upset myself.

I can find a way to say what I want to without anger.

Stay calm—no sarcasm, no attacks.

I can stay calm and relaxed.

Relax and let go. There's no need to get my knickers in a twist.

No one is right, no one is wrong. We just have different needs.

Stay cool, make no judgments.

No matter what is said, I know I'm a good person.

I'll stay rational—anger won't solve anything.

Let them look all foolish and upset. I can stay cool and calm.

Their opinion isn't important. I won't be pushed into losing my cool.

Bottom line, I'm in control. I'm out of here rather than say or do something dumb.

Take a time-out. Cool off, then come back and deal with it.

Some situations don't have good solutions. Looks like this is one of them. No use getting all bent out of shape about it.

It's just a hassle. Nothing more, nothing less. I can cope with hassles.

Break it down. Anger often comes from lumping things together.

Good. I'm getting better at this anger-management stuff.

I got angry but kept the lid on saying dumb things. That's progress.

It's just not worth it to get so angry.

Anger means it's time to relax and cope.

I can manage this; I'm in control.

If they want me to get angry, I'm going to disappoint them.

I can't expect people to act the way I want them to.

I don't have to take this so seriously.

Creating Coping Thoughts

Now you'll create coping thoughts for specific anger triggers. First, write brief descriptions of three recent anger-evoking scenes (different from the three you've already developed). Include everything you see, hear, and feel in the scene, plus your trigger thoughts.

Creating Coping Thoughts Worksheet

Scene A:

Scene B:

Scene C:

Next, break down each anger-evoking scene, as follows.

1. Thoughts that trigger your anger in each scene:

    Scene A: _____

    Scene B: _____

    Scene C: _____

2. Type of trigger thought (blaming, demanding/commanding, etc.)

    Scene A: _____

    Scene B: _____

    Scene C: _____

3. Coping thought(s) for each scene (from trigger-thought countermeasures and General Coping Thoughts List.

    Scene A: _____

    _____

    _____

    Scene B: _____

    _____

    _____

    Scene C: _____

    _____

    _____

Practice Your Anger Relaxation and Restructuring Skills

Before moving on to the final anger-control skill, use the following six steps to combine the skills you've just learned:

1. Visualize Scene A from the Creating Coping Thoughts Worksheet. When you feel moderate anger, erase the scene.

2. Rate your anger level.

3. Practice one relaxation skill (diaphragmatic breathing, relation without tension, or cue-controlled breathing) that works well for you.

4. While relaxing, mentally rehearse the coping thought(s) you prepared for this scene.

5. After 1–2 minutes of relaxing and coping, re-rate your anger level.

6. Repeat the process for Scenes B and C.

Each week, generate three new anger scenes and practice applying the above six steps to each scene. Do this for four weeks (using a total of twelve anger scenes). Many people find it helpful to practice more than once with each scene.

Example. Ray is a social worker who has struggled with externalizing and anger at work. Scene A in his Creating Coping Thoughts Worksheet involved a coworker whose case notes seemed skimpy. While the notes contained basic information social workers typically record, they didn't fully describe the problem or services delivered. First Ray listed the thoughts triggering his anger:

- He's lazy.

- He doesn't care.

- He should document *everything.*

He then identified the type of anger-triggering thoughts:

- Inflammatory global labeling

- Misattribution

- Demanding/commanding

After reviewing countermeasures for his thoughts and the General Coping Thoughts List, Ray settled on these coping thoughts:

- I can't expect people to act the way I want them to.

- His notes aren't as comprehensive as I prefer.

- I can't change him with anger. Time to relax.

Finally, Ray visualized his Scene A, a phone call in which he blew up at his coworker about being lazy, not caring, and writing "worthless" case notes. Ray "heard" what was said, noticed feelings in his body, and recalled his trigger thoughts until he was around 6 on the anger scale. At this point, Ray cut off the scene and practiced cue-controlled breathing interlaced with coping thoughts between breaths. When his anger fell to a 3, Ray moved on to practice his next scene.

Nonviolent Communication

The fourth skill needed to improve your anger control is nonviolent communication—saying what you feel and need in a non-attacking way.

Learning the Three "Fs" of Nonviolent Communication

The key to communicating your needs and feelings without anger is to use the three "Fs"—facts, feelings, and fair requests—in a calm voice.

Facts are a description of the simple, unvarnished event or situation:

- "You were late for meetings three times this week."

- "You haven't shown me your finished homework tonight."

- "The internet has been down since Sunday."

Notice that these facts are expressed without blame or judgment. They are nonpejorative, merely opening a topic for discussion with things you observe—what you see, hear, or notice.

The second "F" is *feelings*. This involves a simple statement of how you feel—taking full responsibility for the emotion without making someone at fault.

- "I feel sad."

- "I feel alone."

- "I feel anxious about your schoolwork."

- "I feel frustrated."

Notice feeling statements aren't phrased as attacks: "I feel that you don't care," "I feel that you're avoiding me." These are judgments cloaked as emotions. Nonviolent expressions of feelings *always* focus on the emotion itself and blame no one for the pain.

The third "F" is *fair requests*. This involves asking for what you want. But the request needs to be specific, behavioral, and doable. Make *one* specific request at a time. Don't ask for everything; just the most important and germane thing to solving the problem. Second, ask for something behavioral. Don't ask for the person to be more loving or make some attitudinal change. Ask them to "Call if you'll be late," "Show me your homework before bedtime," "Please arrive at Zoom meetings before the first item of discussion." Finally, ask for something the other person can *do*—something that's within their power and capacity, something they have control over. Don't ask your partner to like taking steep hikes if they don't, or to not feel attracted to others.

Nonviolent communication has one other component—talking in a calm, uncharged voice. If your words are laden with anger, blame, or disgust, that's all the other person will hear. Keep your tone flat, as conversational as possible.

Rehearsing Nonviolent Communication

Now it's time to visualize and practice the three "Fs" during your anger scenes. The same scenes you developed for anger relaxation and restructuring can now have a new element. After using relaxation (diaphragmatic breathing, relaxation without tension, or cue-controlled breathing) with one or more coping thoughts, you can visualize expressing facts, feelings, and a fair request to whomever triggered your anger. This technique, called *cognitive rehearsal*, allows you to practice nonviolent communication *while feeling some anger*. And it prepares you for real-life situations when someone provokes you because you've already rehearsed a nonviolent response.

Let's check in on Ray. Ray's commitment to anger control led him to sketch out multiple anger scenes and practice both relaxation and anger coping thoughts while feeling upset by the scenes. His last step was to rehearse nonviolent requests for these anger-triggering situations.

Scene A for Ray, if you remember, involved a phone call where he confronted his coworker. Ray identified his three "Fs" for the scene:

- Your notes don't include some things I need to know about this case. (fact)

- I feel anxious that I may not be able to help this client. (feeling)

- Could you fill me in on this case, and in future notes spell out the problem and what you did? (fair request)

Now Ray visualized his phone call, and when his anger reached mid-level, he cut off the scene. He coped with cue-controlled breathing and coping thoughts—bringing his anger down to a 2. At this point he visualized using nonviolent communication, including the facts, his feelings, and a request—all spoken in a calm, uncharged voice. Expressing his feelings and needs without blame helped Ray feel even less triggered. As he rehearsed nonviolent requests in additional scenes, Ray began to feel increasingly confident as he faced anger triggers in real life.

Processes That Increase Compassion

Now that you may be feeling calmer, happier, and more in control by reducing your tendency to blame others, we'll take this to the next level: increasing compassion. *Opposite action* is a valuable skill that's easy to understand and sometimes difficult to accomplish: whatever your painful emotions normally urge you to do, *do the opposite.* Doing the opposite doesn't make you a phony or invalidate your feelings. Your feelings—all of them—are legitimate and valid. But you can choose not to act on them. You can choose to change emotion-driven behaviors that have been damaging your relationships. Opposite action is a way of regulating your feelings, not denying them. It's a way of acknowledging your experience but choosing new behavior to modulate or change how you feel and react.

Doing the same thing you've been doing in response to painful feelings usually intensifies those feelings. Acting on anger with loud accusations might feel good for a moment, but in the long run it damages relationships and leads to more anger, not less. On the other hand, acting contrary to your emotional urges tends to decrease the intensity of emotions. When you feel angry but respond by acknowledging the other person's point of view and speaking in a softer tone of voice, you short-circuit your anger cycle.

Anger's opposite action includes three key behaviors:

- *Validation:* appreciating the other person's pain, problem, or need. If you don't know what the provoking person's problems or needs are, you can ask and then validate by repeating it back in your own words. "I understand, you're feeling anxious about being delayed." "I understand, you had a big disappointment at work and you're feeling kind of shut down." "I understand, you're pretty stressed and would rather rest than do what we planned."

- *Kindness:* concern about, or an actual offer to help with, the other person's problem or need. Kindness can be expressed as a simple "How are you holding up with _____ (the problem)?" or "How is _____ (the problem) affecting you?" Kindness may also include an offer to help. "Is there something I can do?" or "How can I help?" or "Is there a way I can support you with _____ (the problem)?"

- *Gentleness:* a posture, tone, and facial expression that conveys calm and nonaggression. This can include a smile, nodding, a look of interest or concern, and a soft voice. Gentleness is also conveyed with words that lack harsh or judgmental overtones.

Planning to Do the Opposite

Use this worksheet to look back on three recent anger episodes that involved interactions with others and plan how you might respond differently in the future.

Opposite Action Worksheet

Situation 1 _____

Old	New
Actions/words:	Validation:
	Kindness:
Posture/Gesture:	Gentleness:
Facial Expression:	
Tone of Voice:	

Situation 2_____

Old	New
Actions/words:	Validation:
	Kindness:
Posture/Gesture:	Gentleness:
Facial Expression:	
Tone of Voice:	

Situation 3_____

Old	New
Actions/words:	Validation:
	Kindness:
Posture/Gesture:	
	Gentleness:
Facial Expression:	
Tone of Voice:	

Take a look at Ray's Opposite Action Worksheet.

Situation 1 Son's room is a mess.

Old	New
Actions/words: Grabbing his arm. "Look at this. What's the matter with you? Why can't you do your job?" Posture/Gesture: Towering Facial Expression: Angry Tone of Voice: Shouting	Validation: I guess it's hard to stop having fun and clean up. Kindness: Would it help if I kept you company? Gentleness: Sit down Smiling Soft voice

Situation 2 Martha wants to buy an ugly couch.

Old	New
Actions/words: "You have the worst taste in North America. Why make our living room so ugly?" Walking off in anger. Posture/Gesture: Arms folded Facial Expression: Scowling Tone of Voice: Hissing with anger	Validation: What do you like about the couch? I see what's appealing. Kindness: Could we keep looking if I promise we'll get something you like? Gentleness: Touch Martha's arm Smiling kindly Soft, interested

Situation 3 Rideshare partner is late picking me up—again.

Old	New
Actions/words: Pounding on the dashboard. "You're screwing me at work. Why can't you F'ing get your ass here on time?" Posture/Gesture: Fist pounding Facial Expression: Tight, head shaking Tone of Voice: Menacing	Validation: You have to leave earlier to pick me up—that's hard. Kindness: Is there something we can do to make this work better for you—so I get to work on time? Gentleness: Fold hands peacefully Concerned, curious Soft but clear

Now that you looked backward to identify opposite action for recent anger episodes, it's time to use the same process for any future episode. Duplicate the Opposite Action Worksheet and complete an opposite action plan for every anger upset in the next month. Commit yourself to using validation, kindness, and gentleness—in addition to the three "Fs"—at the first indication of anger.

Replacing Anger with Compassion for Others

A daily compassion meditation aimed both at those you love and those who stir anger is a profoundly effective way to replace anger with compassion.

Practice the following meditation by reading it into your smart phone and, in a comfortable place, listening once a day:

Close your eyes and take a breath; let your breathing fall into a gentle rhythm. (Pause) Say to yourself, "In" on the in-breath and "Out" on the out-breath. (Pause) When thoughts occur, notice the thought and gently return attention to the in and out of your breath. (Pause) "In" on the in-breath and "Out" on the out-breath. (Pause 1 minute)

Now bring the image to mind of someone you love. Think of a time when this person was caught in some form of suffering. (Pause 10 seconds) Put your hand on your heart and notice any feelings there as you think of your loved one's pain. Imagine a compassionate golden light around your heart. (Pause)

Continue to see your loved one as you breathe, and with each exhale imagine the golden light from your heart extending to your loved one. Feel the deep wish that they be free from this suffering. (Pause) While bathing them in golden light, say silently:

May you have happiness.

May you be free from suffering.

May you experience joy and ease.

(Repeat for 1 minute)

Now visualize someone with whom you've been recently angry. *(Pause 5 seconds)* Although. you may have angry feelings toward this person, think about how they've suffered during their life. They have dealt with failures, losses, illnesses, and many forms of pain. Think of a situation in which this person may have suffered. *(Pause 20 seconds)*

Put a hand on your heart and imagine it's surrounded by warmth and golden light. Continue to imagine this person as you breathe into your heart center, and imagine the warmth and golden light extending from your heart to the other, easing their suffering. *(Pause)* Let the golden light extend to them on every exhalation with a deep wish that they be free of suffering. *(Pause)* While bathing them in golden light, say silently:

May you have happiness.

May you be free from suffering.

May you experience joy and ease.

(Repeat for 1 minute)

Compassion for others is a powerful antidote for externalization and anger—and a path to healing the stress, pain, and damaged relationships that anger has brought into your life.

Summary

In this chapter you have explored how you tend to externalize and blame all the pain you feel on other people. You have turned that around and found new sources of compassion for others.

From here, return to the assessment chapter and look at your next highest scores on the Comprehensive Coping Inventory–55. That will tell you which chapter to work on next.

CHAPTER 10

Serenity: From Worry and Rumination to Balanced Thinking

Your high score on section 10 or 11 of the Comprehensive Coping Inventory–55 indicates that you tend to worry about the future or ruminate upon the past. Both are forms of *repetitive negative thinking* that can lead to anxiety and depression.

Our minds have one job: to help us survive threats. To do that our minds try to figure out (1) what went wrong and who's at fault, (2) why things went wrong, and (3) what might go wrong in the future. These mental processes have helped us survive as a species for millennia, but they've become a source of enormous psychological pain for humans in the twenty-first century and have shattered our serenity. This chapter will help you see your thoughts for what they are—a mere product of the mind—and to redirect attention away from thoughts into present moment awareness.

Let's get started.

Repetitive Negative Thinking: What It Is

Repetitive negative thinking is the term most broadly used to describe how the mind gets caught in endless loops of rumination and worry that don't solve or protect us from anything. It drives us instead into deeper levels of pain, depression, and anxiety. Below are the three forms of repetitive negative thinking:

- **Negative judgment:** When something bad has happened—now or in the past—your mind ruminates about who screwed up. You or others. Your mind judges you for your errors and mistakes in an effort to keep you from repeating them. Or it judges others, deeming them at fault, to keep you from feeling a sense of shame and failure. Repetitive self-blame can create chronic depression, while judging others can light the fuse of chronic anger.

- **Negative attribution:** This is the natural attempt we all make to explain why bad things happen. We keep trying to find the cause in hopes that we can control and prevent bad things in the future. We ask, *Why am I so sad?...Why didn't my brother invite me for Thanksgiving?...Why didn't I get a promotion?...Why do I have this pain in my stomach?* The problem is that we don't really know, and our minds make up stories about the causes of our pain. In the end we feel helpless because the causes seem out of our control, or we end up feeling wrong and bad because our mind says we failed in some way.

- **Negative prediction:** Whenever confronted with a threat or uncertainty, the mind will careen into endless scenarios regarding the bad things that *could* happen. It's an attempt to control uncertainty and predict the future. This is worry—the attempt to envision all possible negative outcomes in order to avoid them. It doesn't work. Instead of helping us feel safer and more in control, worry about future catastrophes amps up our alarm system and creates chronic, high levels of anxiety.

Repetitive negative thinking is a maladaptive response to emotional pain and/or threat. It is an attempt to avoid pain or control threats by making negative judgments of yourself or others, by trying to find the cause (attribution), or by predicting and preparing for negative outcomes. While it provides a brief illusion that you can suppress pain or control threats, dozens of studies have linked the coping mechanisms of worry and rumination (repetitive negative thinking) to high levels of anxiety and depression. Cognitive behavior therapy researchers, in hundreds of studies, have shown that our thoughts have a direct influence on our emotions, and that the frequency and duration of negative thinking profoundly impacts our emotional pain.

Processes That Reduce Repetitive Negative Thinking

In this section you'll learn to overcome repetitive negative thinking through a change process called *defusion* (Hayes, Strosahl, and Wilson 1999), which involves noticing your negative thoughts and detaching from them so they're less likely to create or intensify negative feelings. Defusion has been shown to reduce attachment to negative thoughts, reduce anxiety and depression, and increase cognitive flexibility. You'll learn to detach from negative thoughts by first observing and labeling them and then letting them go. The process will help you change your relationship to thoughts, recognizing that they aren't "real" or in most cases important.

Defusion

The best approach to reducing the time spent in negative thinking is defusion. This is because the mind's design as a survival mechanism has some problematic side effects. You tend to automatically trust that your thoughts are true so that you can react quickly to either danger or opportunity. For example, if you see dark and light stripes moving in the grass, your mind converts the sense impression into a language symbol (the word "tiger") and then correlates the symbol with all of your other associations related to tigers and concludes, "Danger!" This thought causes a flight response in your body, so you run away. If that movement in the grass is actually a tiger, that's clearly an upside of how the mind works.

The problem is that many thoughts aren't accurate. Sometimes your sense impressions are wrong: it's actually a chipmunk or the wind in the grass, not a tiger. Unfortunately, the mind manipulates symbols as if they were reality. Perhaps, years ago, you had a bad experience involving a stranger, a car accident, or your mother. Since then, your mind has been making associations to that experience until finally you may distrust all strangers, fear driving, or hate all tall, blonde women because your mind has associated them with your mother.

Because it's a way of taking time out from believing everything your mind comes up with, defusion is a shortcut to serenity. When you defuse, you step aside from the fire hose of thoughts that are pushing you around. You put in the clutch to disengage from the constantly running motor of your mind so that it stops driving you down the road to depression, anxiety, and other difficult emotions.

When you can stop identifying with negative thoughts and begin observing them in the context of the many other thoughts and feelings you experience, negative appraisals will become much less powerful and less frequent. And when you dismiss the thoughts that lead to rumination about the past or worry about the future as "just another thought," you stop the process of rumination and worry in its tracks.

Try each of these exercises in turn; they will give you a good feel for how your mind creates and processes the meaning of words, and how thoughts and images flow through your awareness.

Milkmilkmilk

This exercise is a language game that shows how meaning attaches to and detaches from words. It was originally created by British psychologist Edward Titchener (1916) and is now widely used in acceptance and commitment therapy. It's very simple.

Find a private place where you can speak without any concern about being overheard.

Close your eyes for a moment and imagine that you're opening a container of fresh, cold milk. Feel the texture of the container, then imagine pouring some milk into a glass. See the white, creamy stream bubble up and fill the glass. Smell the milk, then take a sip. Dwell on this sequence until it becomes very clear to you. At this point, you probably have the faint taste of milk in your mouth, even though you aren't actually drinking any milk. That's because your mind's incredible ability to code sense impressions into symbols works backward as well: it can turn symbols like the word "milk" into imaginary sense impressions.

Now you'll temporarily turn off this mechanism for coding sense impressions into symbols—and vice-versa—for the word "milk." Say the word "milk" out loud, over and over again. Say it as fast as you can while still pronouncing it clearly. Time yourself and do it for 20 to 45 seconds.

What happened to the meaning of the word? Most likely, the word "milk" became a nonsense sound for you, no longer calling up vivid sense impressions of the wet, cold, creamy substance you've known all your life. Did you notice that the word started sounding odd? Did you start focusing on the way your mouth and jaw muscles moved or how the end of one repetition of the word transitioned into the beginning of the next?

Most people find that the meaning of the word "milk" fades after repeating the word for a while. This fading of meaning rarely happens in real life. We're all so immersed in a stream of talk and words that we rarely notice that they're just a bunch of sounds.

Negative Label Repetition

In this exercise you'll apply the milkmilkmilk effect to one of the negative labels you tend to apply to yourself. As in the previous exercise, find a private place where you can speak without any concern about being overheard. Start by summing up a negative thought you have about yourself into one word. Pick a really harsh, emotionally loaded, negative word, like "stupid," "loser," "wimp," "bully," "worthless," "coward," or "failure." A one- or two-syllable word is best; the shorter the word, the better this approach will work. Write the word you've chosen on a piece of paper. Rate how painful or distressing it is to think that this word applies to you, using a scale of 0 to 10, where 0 means no pain at all and 10 means maximally painful. Then rate how true or believable the word seems to you at this moment, using a scale of 0 to 10, in which 0 means not believable at all, and 10 means totally true and accurate.

Now repeat the word out loud for 20 to 45 seconds, just like you did the word "milk." Notice how much meaning detached from your negative word. Did it become less painful? Did it start to become less true or believable? Rate your word again to see how much it changed in terms of how painful (0 to 10) and how true (0 to 10).

Leaves on a Stream

This is a classic meditation practice, used in various forms all over the world, to quiet and clear the mind. Find a quiet place to practice where you won't be disturbed.

Sit down, close your eyes, and imagine that you're sitting on the bank of a slow-moving stream on a warm, peaceful autumn day. Occasionally a leaf falls into the water and floats away on the current, drifting out of sight downstream. Give yourself enough time to form a clear picture of the scene.

Start noticing your thoughts. Whenever a thought comes to mind, sum it up in a single word or phrase: "boring"…"Johnny"…"sad"…"dumb exercise"…"what's for lunch?"…and so on.

Put your word or phrase on a leaf and let it float away, out of sight and out of mind.

If thoughts arise as images, without specific words, then place the images on the leaf and let them float away.

Don't try to make the current flow faster or slower, and don't try to change what's on the leaves in any way. Don't worry if the stream won't flow or if you find yourself stuck on a leaf along with a thought or image. And don't be surprised or worried if the leaves disappear, the whole scene disappears, or you go somewhere else mentally. Just notice that these things happen and then return to the scene beside the stream.

Keep doing this for about 5 minutes. This should give you enough time to have the experience of trying to let go of your thoughts.

This exercise can exemplify how sticky some thoughts are. They can grab you and take you along for a ride even when your intention is entirely otherwise. But this exercise also gives you some practice in letting go of thoughts and letting them drift away. When the stream wouldn't flow or you were stuck on a leaf with your thoughts, you were experiencing *fusion* with your thoughts. When the stream was flowing freely and the leaves carried your thoughts out of sight, you were experiencing *defusion*.

White Room Meditation

This is a meditation technique for observing thoughts as they pass through your mind. Again, find a quiet place to practice where you won't be disturbed.

Sit down, close your eyes, and imagine that your mind is an empty white room with two doors. Watch as your thoughts enter through one door and leave through the other.

As each thought crosses the room, dispassionately observe and label it: "jealousy"… "depressing thought"…"thought about Joan"…"mother"…"guilty thought"…and so on. Notice when thoughts don't quickly leave the white room and instead hang around in your mind. This happens when you start buying into or believing your thoughts. If you have trouble letting go of a sticky thought, move your attention to the door through which new thoughts emerge and just wait for the next thought.

This exercise gives you practice in labeling or categorizing your thoughts, a key skill for doing the real-life defusion exercises in the next section.

Real-Life Defusion Exercises

In your day-to-day life, you can't walk around saying "milkmilkmilk" or periodically drop into the lotus position on the sidewalk to meditate. You need shorter, simpler defusion exercises that you can do in an elevator, on the bus, in a meeting, on an airplane, in the shower, in your car, or wherever you find yourself. Here are some approaches you can use in your day-to-day life.

What's My Mind Up To?

This technique helps you defuse from your thoughts by creating some analytical distance. When you feel distressed, try this simple technique: instead of dwelling on distressing thoughts, ask yourself, "What's my mind up to?" Then answer yourself by labeling each thought as your mind presents it:

"Now my mind is having a _____ thought."

Repeat this sentence until you've labeled five to ten thoughts. You'll find that most distressing thoughts fit into the categories of worry and judgment, so you shouldn't have to search very long for the right word to fill in the blanks.

Labeling Thoughts

Notice that instead of using statements like "Now I'm worried" or "Now I'm worrying," the previous exercises use the phrasing, "Now my mind is having a [worry] thought." This is labeling: describing a thought as something your mind produces rather than something you are or something you do. It's a subtle distinction, but it lies at the heart of defusion. There are a variety of other ways you can label your experiences. When you have a distressing thought, feeling, or urge, try labeling it using one of these forms:

- I am having the thought that _____ (describe your thought).

- I'm having the feeling that _____ (describe your emotion).

- I'm having a memory of _____ (describe your memory).

- I am feeling the body sensation of _____ (describe your body sensation).

- I am noticing a desire to _____ (describe your behavioral urge).

Circumlocution

The labels above are circumlocutions—longer, wordier descriptions of your thoughts, sensations, or urges that take your mind off of automatic pilot and cast your assessments as transient creations of your mind, rather than as true facts about you or the world. Circumlocution helps you separate yourself from your mind and also dilute your interior monologue with extra verbiage, slowing down your stream of consciousness so that you can see what your mind is up to.

You can make up your own circumlocutions to defuse from fast, short, sharply painful thoughts. For example, *I'm anxious* might become *My mind is once again having that very familiar thought that I am anxious.* Likewise, *Asshole!* might become *I notice that my mind is having a hateful thought about Jim and calling him an asshole.*

"Thank You, Mind"

In this very brief defusion technique, you simply thank your mind every time an unpleasant thought pops up. It's a quick way of reminding yourself that it's only a thought, that thinking is what your mind does, and that in a minute your mind will be doing something else. It may take several thank you's to defuse from a persistent train of thought. Here's an example:

What I said was lame. "Thank you, mind."

I'm a loser. "Thank you, mind."

They're laughing at me. "Thank you, mind."

I'm anxious. "Thank you, mind."

I'm dizzy. "Thank you, mind."

After sufficient thank you's, your mind will say, *Oh, alright, never mind.*

Turning a Hand

Each time you have a painful thought, let go of it by turning your hand over as if you're letting go of a small stone that you've been carrying. Tell yourself, *There's a thought…let it go,* as you turn a hand and let the thought fall away.

Breathe and Let Go

Each time you have a painful thought, take a deep breath and, as you release the breath, imagine that the thought is being let go with the breath. Tell yourself, *There's a thought,* (and as you breathe it out) *let it go.*

Card Carrying

Write your most typical bothersome thoughts on a 3 x 5 index card and carry it in your pocket or purse. When your mind comes up with one of these thoughts, dismiss it by saying to yourself, *I've got it on the card.* You don't need to once again dwell on past mistakes, worry about a potential confrontation, or catalog your shortcomings. You've already done those things, and you've got them on the card.

Techniques for Sticky or Frequently Encountered Negative Thoughts

Negative thoughts are sticky, often to the point we feel mentally glued to them. The following techniques will help you change your relationship to particular and chronic negative thoughts by examining how old they are, their function, and their workability.

"How Old Is This Thought?"

Each time you have a familiar painful thought, ask yourself, *How old is this?* Recall the earliest time you can remember having the thought. This will remind you that it's just a thought, that it has come up before, that it will continue to come up from time to time, and that you will continue to survive the thought and carry on with your life, just as you always have before.

Some old thoughts have happened hundreds, or even thousands, of times. It can be helpful to make a rough estimate of how many times your mind has produced this particular thought.

"What's That Thought in the Service Of?"

When intrusive thoughts plague you, ask yourself, *What's that in the service of? What is my mind trying to get me to do?* For instance, say your husband's birthday is coming up, and you know he'd like to go out to dinner at his favorite restaurant, but every time you think about making reservations, you remember hearing about a mugging not too far from the restaurant and think, *What if we get mugged?* A wave of anxiety and depression hits you, and you feel overwhelmed.

The next time it happens, ask yourself, *What's that in the service of? What is my mind trying to get me to do?…And what is my mind trying to protect me from?* The fact is, maybe you almost never go out at night because it makes you nervous to be away from home after dark. In that case you'd realize that your thoughts are in the service of immobilizing you until it's too late to make a reservation. And in answer to the question about what your mind is trying to protect you from, the answer might be, *It's trying to protect me from danger and feeling unsafe.* Seeing the function of an intrusive thought—an attempt to protect you from a painful emotion or from doing something that feels dangerous—is very different from buying into the thought. When you buy into a thought, you're assuming it's true. When you see the purpose of a thought, you realize it's just your mind trying to make you do or not do something or protect you from some emotional pain.

"And How Has That Thought Worked for Me?"

This exercise continues the theme of the previous one. If you have the thought, *What if we get mugged?* and feel paralyzed whenever you consider going out at night, ask yourself, *And how has that thought worked for me?* Chances are, it's worked to keep you stuck at home alone while your partner or friends go out without you, and your life has diminished over time as a result. If the thought was trying to protect you from an emotion, like anxiety or the sense of danger, you can ask the same question: *How has that worked?* Do you feel less anxious and less unsafe because of the thought?

By asking, *And how has this thought worked for me?* you expose the consequences of *being* your thoughts, as opposed to *having* your thoughts. You gain a bit of distance from your thoughts and throw some light into the space between what you think and who you are.

The Defusion Drill

To wrap up this section, we'll combine a few of the defusion techniques you've learned:

- Notice the thought. Sometimes the first thing you notice is the emotional pain produced by the negative thought. Be aware of the first touch of depression or anxiety, and look for the thought behind it.

- Label the thought. "I am having a _____ thought."

- Let go of the thought—by turning the hand, taking a breath and letting it go, thanking your mind, card carrying, or any "float-away" visualization (e.g., Leaves on a Stream, described above; imagining balloons carrying each thought and floating away in the sky; thoughts as billboards you pass while driving; thoughts as pop-ups on your computer).

- Ask these three questions: (1) Is this thought helpful? (2) Do I need to think about it now? (3) What would I prefer doing with this moment? For particularly sticky or repetitive thoughts, ask these questions instead: (1) How old is the thought? (2) What is the purpose or function of the thought? (3) How has that thought worked for me?

Processes That Increase Balanced Thinking

While defusion helps you reduce the time spent in negative thinking, balanced thinking can help you develop the mental muscle to shift focus and attend to something else. In this section you'll learn the change process of *attentional flexibility*—the ability to shift focus from negative thoughts to awareness of the present moment. Attentional flexibility (Wells 2009; Kabat-Zinn 1990; Hayes and Smith 2005) has been shown to reduce worry and rumination while increasing mindfulness and quality of life. Once you have a handle on attentional flexibility, you'll learn how to practice mindfulness in your daily life and, ultimately, to choose your mind's focus—all necessary components of balanced thinking.

Attentional Flexibility

There are various ways to increase your attentional flexibility and shift your mind to the present moment. We'll start with one of the most common.

Mindful Meditation

This practice will teach you how to observe the three aspects of inner experience—thoughts, sensations, and emotions—while also learning to shift attention back to your breath. You'll become skilled at watching, without judgment, your inner experience and strengthening your ability to move your awareness to something else. Record the following 10-minute script on your phone and listen once daily:

Arrange your body in a comfortable position and close your eyes. (*Pause 10 seconds*)

Let your attention drop to your diaphragm—the center of your breath—and notice the experience of breathing. (*Pause*) Say to yourself, "In" on the in-breath and "Out" on the out-breath. (*Pause*) Just noting in and out for each breath. (*Pause 10 seconds*) Right now try to stay with your breath. If your attention moves to other things, gently return your focus to your breath. (*Pause 30 seconds*)

Now, for a moment, bring your attention to your inner experience. Notice if there is a sensation somewhere in your body. (*Pause*) Observe without judging it and let it be what it is. (*Pause 10 seconds*) Now say to yourself, "Feeling," and bring your awareness back to the in and out of your breath. (*Pause 10 seconds*)

Now, for a moment, bring your attention to any emotion you may feel. (*Pause*) Observe the emotion without judging it and let it be what it is. (*Pause 10 seconds*) Now say to yourself, "Emotion," and bring your awareness back to the in and out of your breath. (*Pause 10 seconds*)

Now, for a moment, bring your attention to any thoughts you may have. (*Pause*) Observe your thought without judgment and let it be what it is. (*Pause 10 seconds*) Now say to yourself, "Thought," and gently bring your awareness back to the in and out of your breath. (*Pause 10 seconds*)

Now let your awareness roam across your inner experience. If you notice a thought, observe it for a moment, and say to yourself, "Thought." Then bring your attention back to your breath. (*Pause*) If you notice an emotion, observe it for a moment and say, "Emotion." Then bring your attention back to your breath. (*Pause*) If you notice a sensation, observe it for a moment and say, "Feeling." Then bring your attention back to your breath. (*Pause 1 minute*)

Keep observing your inner experience. If you notice a thought, say, "Thought," and return to your breath. If you notice an emotion, say, "Emotion," and return to your breath. If you notice a sensation, say, "Feeling," and return to your breath. (*Pause 1 minute*)

Now firmly anchor attention to your breath. Say "In" on the in-breath and "Out" on the out-breath. If your attention moves elsewhere, gently and immediately return focus to your breath. (*Pause 30 seconds*)

In a moment, when you're ready, take a deep breath and open your eyes. Look around and bring your full awareness to your surroundings.

Practice Mindful Meditation daily until you feel able to observe your inner experience without judgment and can easily switch attention from thoughts, feelings, or emotions to your breath during meditation.

Attention-Switching Meditation

This practice of attention switching will strengthen your ability to switch from thinking mode to observing mode, from worry and rumination to watching the present moment. Record the following 5-minute script on your phone and listen twice daily:

Arrange your body in a comfortable position, eyes open. Take several deep breaths to release tension. (*Pause 20 seconds*)

Right now turn your attention to your thoughts; just watch the parade of thoughts without judging or clinging to any of them. Just watch. (*Pause 30 seconds*)

Now switch your attention to sensations inside your body. Just watch these feelings without judgment or any attempt at control. (*Pause 30 seconds*)

Now turn your attention back to your thoughts, just watching the parade without judging or clinging to any of them. (*Pause 30 seconds*)

Now switch your attention to your emotions, just watching whatever's there without judgment or any attempt at control. You don't have to name the emotion, just watch. (*Pause 30 seconds*)

Now turn your attention back to your thoughts, just watching the parade without judging or clinging to any of them. (*Pause 30 seconds*)

Now switch your attention to your outside experience—what you see, hear, smell, or touch. (*Pause 30 seconds*)

Now back to your thoughts. (*10 seconds*) Switch to your inner sensations. (*10 seconds*) Back to noticing your thoughts. (*10 seconds*) Switch to noticing emotions. (*10 seconds*) Back to your thoughts. (*10 seconds*) Switch now to your outer experience (what you see, hear, smell, touch). (*10 seconds*)

Now back to your thoughts. (*10 seconds*) Switch to your inner sensations. (*10 seconds*) Back to noticing your thoughts. (*10 seconds*) Switch to noticing emotions. (*10 seconds*) Back to your thoughts. (*10 seconds*) Switch to your outer experience (what you see, hear, smell, touch). (*10 seconds*)

You'll find that some thoughts are quite sticky, and it takes some effort and time to switch to observing other experiences. That's okay. With practice it will get easier. Your mental muscle will strengthen. The rapid switching (10 seconds) portion of the meditation, while sometimes tiring, is especially useful for building the mental muscle to move your mind from repetitive negative thoughts to the experience of the moment.

Five Senses Exercise

An easy portal to the present moment is to catalog what each of your senses is telling you. Spend about 30 seconds focusing on what you see, then another 30 seconds or so on anything you can smell. Move on to what you hear, then any sensations of taste, and finally any tactile sensations originating both inside and outside your body, spending about 30 seconds with each. The entire exercise can be completed in 2 to 3 minutes. But here's the most important part: every time a thought pops into your mind, notice it and then bring your attention back to whatever sense you're observing. The point of the exercise isn't to stop your thought: your mind will keep chattering, no matter what. The point is to let thoughts go, rather than getting caught up in long chains of judgments and what-if thoughts.

The Five Senses Exercise is a great way to take a break from worries. As soon as you've been pulled into a worry rut, just shift to what you're seeing right now, and then what you're smelling, hearing, and so on. By the time you get through checking in with your five senses, you may not feel much need to go back to that old painful thinking.

Mindfulness of the Present Moment in Daily Life

The more you stay in the present moment, the less you'll worry and ruminate. To begin integrating mindfulness into your daily life, choose to apply it to something you do briefly every day. It could be taking a shower, doing the dishes, drinking coffee, walking to the bus stop, eating breakfast, or helping your children get dressed. The activity should be physical, not mental, so you can focus on each detail of the experience. For example, if you've chosen doing the dishes as an opportunity for daily mindfulness, you'd try to focus on the feeling of hot water on your hands. You'd notice sensations of holding the sponge and feeling the slippery soap. Then you'd pay attention to the texture of the dish in your hands and the sensation of water as you rinse it.

It doesn't matter what activity you choose. The point is to listen to what all your senses tell you. What you see, hear, feel, smell, and taste are the cornerstones of mindfulness. When thoughts intrude, notice and label them, then return your attention to the sensory details of the activity you've chosen.

Practice doing your activity mindfully for a week. Sometimes it helps to put up signs or reminders to cue you to do the exercise. For example, a plan to do the dishes mindfully is more likely to happen if you put a sign over the sink. A plan to eat breakfast mindfully would be supported by a sign on the refrigerator, a carton of milk, or something else you typically consume at breakfast. If you plan to take a mindful walk to the bus stop, tie a piece of string on your briefcase or backpack as a reminder.

After the first week, add a second mindful activity and use a similar reminder system to help you follow through. Continue to add new mindful activities to your routine every week until you have a number of them peppered throughout your day.

While all mindfulness exercises will help you reduce negative thinking, you will still have moments when painful thoughts show up. Whenever that happens, slow down, make sure you're doing just one thing, and then pay attention to the physical activity you're engaged in. Try to notice only that activity and nothing else. Let yourself get immersed in what you're doing by paying attention to what your eyes, ears, and other senses tell you.

Doing one thing at a time helps slow you down and quiet your thoughts; it will help you shift from thoughts about the future and the past to what's happening right now.

Choosing Your Mind's Focus

With more flexible thinking skills, you can choose what you think about. When negative thoughts show up, your first choice is "Now or later." If the thought feels compelling and you choose to think about it now, so be it. Any time you get tired of the thought, you can use defusion skills to let go and make room for another focus. You can also delay worry and rumination, setting a later time for those thoughts (writing them down to make sure you don't forget).

The next choice is what your alternative focus will be. Usually the best alternative focus is the present moment. Paying attention to your experience right now—everything your senses tell you about this moment—precludes worry and rumination. Other choices for an alternative mental focus include:

- planning
- problem solving
- pleasant reminiscing
- daydreaming about positive future events
- creative activities
- pleasure activities

- exercise

- reading and learning

- communicating and connecting

Remember, you control where your attention goes—so choose a focus that promote your mental well-being!

Summary

You have learned in this chapter that you can't completely banish negative thoughts. From time to time they will get triggered. But you can significantly reduce repetitive negative thinking and choose what to do when a negative thought shows up. You can defuse from the thought, let it go, and choose another focus for your mind.

From here, return to the assessment chapter and look at your next highest scores on the Comprehensive Coping Inventory–55. That will tell you which chapter to work on next.

CHAPTER 11

Relapse Prevention

Occasionally slipping back into your old ways of dealing with painful emotions is inevitable. The skills you've learned in this book work well, but they aren't a "single-dose" solution like penicillin or the polio vaccine. Sometimes you need a booster shot: another round of consciously and purposely practicing your new ways of coping with stress.

Because you're bound to experience the occasional relapse from time to time, it makes sense to have a plan for what to do about it. That way you can promptly get back on an even keel emotionally and spend as little time as possible in distress. This chapter will help you draft such a plan.

Step 1: List Your Warning Signs

The first step is to recognize the signs of relapse. How do you know when you've relapsed, anyway? If you were trying to stop smoking or drinking, relapse would be obvious: it happens whenever you smoke or drink again. But relapse in the emotional realm is more subtle. It can sneak up on you if you're not alert for the signs that you're slipping back into your old habitual ways of thinking and acting.

Below are common warning signs to be on the lookout for:

Red Flag Emotions

By this point in the book, you should have a pretty good idea of what your red flag emotions are. Still, take a moment to list the feelings that bother you the most and that you have the most trouble dealing with:

_____

_____

_____

High-Risk Situations

Now consider your high-risk situations. In what circumstances are you most likely to experience your red flag emotions? Where are you? Who are you with? What's happening? In the space below, make a list of the people, places, and activities that are most likely to trigger problematic feelings:

_____

_____

_____

Rigid Coping Mechanisms

What do you do when your emotions are driving you? Review your scores from the Comprehensive Coping Inventory–55 in the assessment chapter. If it's been a long time since you completed the assessment, do it again. Note here your most troublesome coping mechanisms:

- ☐ Behavioral avoidance
- ☐ Safety seeking
- ☐ Emotion-driven behavior
- ☐ Distress intolerance
- ☐ Emotion avoidance
- ☐ Thought avoidance
- ☐ Cognitive misappraisals
- ☐ Self-blame
- ☐ Blaming others
- ☐ Worry
- ☐ Rumination

Rumination, Worry, and Negative Appraisals

What are you thinking about when you experience intense, painful feelings? What's going through your mind and bringing up those feelings over and over or prolonging them for hours or days? What past events do you ruminate about? What future possibilities do you worry about? What negative labels do you habitually apply to your experience? Write your usual topics for rumination, worry, and negative appraisal here:

_____

_____

_____

Avoidance and Suppression

How do you try to avoid or suppress painful feelings? Do you limit your life by staying away from certain people, places, or activities? Do you try to keep your mind blank or numb? Do you try to keep painful feelings at bay with certain repetitive mental rituals? In the space below, list the ways you most typically try to avoid or suppress your feelings:

_____

_____

_____

Example. Emily, a recently divorced forty-six-year-old teacher, had two teenage children whom she worried about a lot. She was behind on her bills and also worried about her mother, who was becoming more and more forgetful and irritable. Here is how Emily listed her warning signs:

Red Flag Emotions

Anxiety, guilt, depression

High-Risk Situations

Visiting Mom

When my kids are away from home

Paying bills

Rigid Coping Mechanisms

Blaming Others: Fussing and nagging at Mom

Safety seeking: Calling kids' cell phones too much

Emotion-driven behavior: Overspending on the credit card

Rumination, Worry, and Negative Appraisals

My wild, reckless youth

Envisioning my kids being assaulted or in getting in car wrecks

Bankruptcy, not having a place to live, and thinking "I'm a failure"

Avoidance and Suppression

Keeping the TV on all the time

Postponing visits to Mom

Procrastinating on the bills

Step 2: Review and Practice Your Skills

The most important step in dealing with a relapse is recognizing that you're having a relapse. Once you realize that you're in a high-risk situation, are starting to experience red flag emotions, and are returning to some previous negative thinking patterns, you can revisit some of the earlier chapters to reinforce the skills you've learned in this book:

- End behavioral avoidance by moving into action and engagement with others (chapter 1).

- Have the courage to stop safety-seeking behaviors and rely on your new sense of inner safety (chapter 2).

- Change emotion-driven reactions into values-driven choices (chapter 3).

- Push past your distress intolerance to an acceptance of the inevitable pain in life (chapter 4).

- Move through emotion avoidance to acceptance and openness about your feelings (chapter 5).

- Shift from thought avoidance to thought acceptance (chapter 6).

- Escape your cognitive misappraisals (i.e., habitual thinking traps) by thinking flexibly (chapter 7).

- Soften self-blame with self-compassion (chapter 8).

- Replace blaming others with expressions of compassion (chapter 9).

- Replace worry and rumination (i.e., repetitive negative thinking) with balanced thinking (chapter 10).

Conclusion

Although occasional relapses are inevitable, they are also transient. By being alert to the signs that you're slipping back into ineffective ways of reacting to painful emotions, you can quickly get back on track by applying the skills you've learned in this book.

Congratulations for having the courage and persistence to work hard on healing your emotional pain.

The Comprehensive Coping Index–55

The Comprehensive Coping Index–55 (CCI-55; Zurita Ona 2007; Pool 2021) is a fifty-five-item questionnaire that helps assess sixteen "transdiagnostic mechanisms," or problematic coping processes. It was designed to be used in clinical settings with individuals who report struggling with mental health issues to assist in pinpointing what interventions might help those individuals. It has been validated, further developed, and researched since its creation.

History of the CCI

The original CCI, created by McKay and Zurita Ona in 2007, attempted to capture a very wide range of coping behaviors (Zurita Ona 2007), which were then condensed into seven subscales, called "transdiagnostic factors." Later research continued to develop the CCI by combining, refining, and adding new processes based on the most useful and relevant transdiagnostic mechanisms being studied in the field of psychology.

In 2012, Ahrendt reviewed the CCI in a doctoral dissertation that validated the measure's reliability and usefulness, comparing the results of the CCI to a very well-accepted measure of depression, anxiety, and stress. This research found a significant relationship between the CCI and symptoms of depression, anxiety, and stress, supporting the hypothesis that participants who report engaging in response mechanisms captured by the CCI are more likely to experience depression, stress, and anxiety (Ahrendt 2012).

In 2014, the CCI was revised to reflect modern research and thinking about transdiagnostic mechanisms, resulting in the CCI-R. McKay and Zurita Ona expanded the measure to match the sixteen "response mechanisms" presented in *The Transdiagnostic Road Map to Case Formulation and Treatment Planning*, Frank and Davidson's 2014 practical guide to a number of mechanisms that underlie and maintain psychological problems.

In 2015, Birnbaum conducted an in-depth statistical assessment of the new CCI-R to test for reliability. The study also explored how well the CCI-R is able to differentiate between people who are struggling with mental health issues and those who are not (Birnbaum 2015). Birnbaum found that eleven of the sixteen variables were able to distinguish between individuals struggling with mental health issues and those who were not.

In 2017, Frazier further validated the CCI-R, finding moderate to strong correlations between CCI-R subscales and many other, well-researched measures of similar concepts. Overall, this research found that the CCI-R measures the processes that it claims to measure (Frazier 2017).

In 2020, Pool evaluated the CCI-R to make sure all of the processes being measured were able to distinguish between individuals struggling with mental health issues and those who were not (Pool 2021). This research evaluated the CCI-R on a more culturally representative sample. Pool also further revised the CCI-R to reduce repetitive subscales, resulting in a more efficient measure called the CCI-55.

Research Supporting the Current CCI-55

The CCI-55 was tested on a sample of 383 adults, ages 18–85 years old, using an online data-collection tool called Mechanical Turk (Pool 2021). It was tested for construct validity, internal consistency, clinical utility, and generalizability across demographics and cultural identities. The 55-item scale was found to have satisfactory construct validity, and all eleven subscales were found to have good internal consistency and clinical utility. The following analyses further supported the CCI-55's usefulness:

1. **Content Validity.** Expert ratings of the items and subscales, performed by ten area experts in transdiagnostic mechanisms, were found to be above 75% accuracy for content validity and above a 3.0 out of 4 for subjective quality of items. *This suggests that the CCI-55 is useful for measuring each of the processes it is supposed to measure.*

2. **Reliability and internal consistency.** The subscales of the CCI-55, many of which were created from combinations of CCI-R subscales, performed well in terms of internal consistency as measured by Cronbach's alpha. Each subscale's internal consistency was above the typical threshold of .75. *This means that the items that measure each of the processes in the CCI-55 are similar enough to be useful, without being so similar that they are redundant.*

3. **Clinical Utility and Clinical Cutoffs.** *T*-tests and ANOVAs were conducted to compare CCI-55 results across groups of participants based on their self-reported mental health struggles. *These analyses support the idea that the CCI-55 is sensitive enough to measure the differences in coping styles between people who report struggling with mental health issues and those who do not report struggling.* The strong effect size for these analyses suggests that this difference is clinically relevant. Further, in order to create suggested guidelines for use of the CCI-55, *T*-scores were derived based on how individuals struggling with mental health issues responded to the subscales compared to how individuals who were not struggling responded. *This created "cut-off scores" to help determine what scores for each process should be considered "elevated" or problematic.*

4. **Generalizability.** A more culturally diverse sample was collected for the CCI-55. Respondents were 37% White/European, 26% Black, 18% Latinx, 16% Asian, 4% Indigenous, 2% South East Asian, 1% Middle Eastern, and 2% Other. The measure performed equally well across demographics as measured by statistical comparisons, with the following exceptions: cisgendered men scored significantly higher on Emotion Avoidance than cisgendered women and gender-expansive individuals, and gender-expansive individuals scored higher on Emotion-Driven Behavior and Externalizing than cisgendered women. In addition, older adults scored lower overall on the CCI-55 than younger adults.

To date, this most recent CCI-55 remains the most comprehensive measure of transdiagnostic response mechanisms available and is currently used in several community clinics and outpatient settings. It is used to assess how people cope with difficulty, to provide guidance for intervention, and to track progress over time.

References

Ahrendt, T. M. 2012. "Coping and the Transdiagnostic Approach: A Symbiotic Relationship? Validating the Comprehensive Coping Index for Clinical Use and Further Research." Dissertation, The Wright Institute.

Allen, L. B., R. K. McHugh, and D. B. Barlow. 2008. "Emotional Disorders: A Unified Protocol." In *Clinical Handbook of Psychological Disorders*, edited by D. H. Barlow. New York: Guilford Press.

Astin, J. A. 1997. "Stress Reduction Through Mindfulness Meditation: Effects on Psychological Symptomatology, Sense of Control, and Spiritual Experiences." *Psychotherapy and Psychosomatics* 66(2): 97–106. https://doi.org/10.1159/000289116

Barlow, D. H., L. B. Allen, and M. L. Choate. 2004. "Toward a Unified Treatment of Emotional Disorders." *Behavior Therapy* 35(2): 205–230.

Beck, A. T., A. J. Rush, B. F. Shaw, and G. Emery. 1979. *Cognitive Therapy of Depression*. New York: Guilford Press.

Berenbaum, H., C. Raghavan, H.-N. Le, L. L. Vernon, and J. J. Gomez. 2003. "A Taxonomy of Emotional Disturbances." *Clinical Psychology: Science and Practice* 10(2): 206–226.

Birnbaum, A. P. 2015. "Approaching Transdiagnostically: A Validation Study of the Comprehensive Coping Inventory." Dissertation, The Wright Institute.

Blaustein, M. E., and K. M. Kinniburgh. 2017. "Attachment, Self-Regulation, and Competency (ARC)." In *Evidence-Based Treatments For Trauma-Related Disorders in Children And Adolescents*, edited by U. Schnyder and M. Cloitre. Cham, Switzerland: Springer.

Chambers, R., B. C. Y. Lo, and N. B. Allen. 2008. "The Impact of Intensive Mindfulness Training on Attentional Control, Cognitive Style, and Affect." *Cognitive Therapy and Research* 32: 303–322. https://doi.org/10.1007/s10608-007-9119-0

Cloninger, C. R. 1999. "A New Conceptual Paradigm from Genetics and Psychobiology for the Science of Mental Health." *Australian and New Zealand Journal of Psychiatry* 33: 174–186.

Craske, M. G., and G. Simos. 2013. "Panic Disorder and Agoraphobia." In *CBT For Anxiety Disorders: A Practitioner Book*, edited by G. Simos and S. G. Hofmann. Hoboken, NJ: Wiley-Blackwell.

Craske, M. G., M. Treanor, C. C. Conway, T. Zbozinek, and B. Vervliet. 2014. "Maximizing Exposure Therapy: an Inhibitory Learning Approach." *Behaviour Research and Therapy* 58: 10–23.

Davidson, R. J., J. Kabat-Zinn, J. Schumacher, M. Rosenkranz, D. Muller, S. F. Santorelli, F. Urbanowski, A. Harrington, K. Bonus, and J. F. Sheridan. 2003. "Alterations in Brain and Immune Function Produced by Mindfulness Meditation." *Psychosomatic Medicine* 65(4): 564–570.

De Castella, K., M. J. Platow, M. Tamir, and J. J. Gross. 2018. "Beliefs About Emotion: Implications for Avoidance-Based Emotion Regulation and Psychological Health." *Cognition and Emotion* 32(4): 773–795.

Deffenbacher, J. L. 1988. "Cognitive-Relaxation and Social Skills Treatment of Anger." *Journal of Counseling Psychology* 35: 234–236.

Deffenbacher, J. L. 1993. "General Anger: Characteristics and Clinical Implications." *Psicologia Conductual* 1: 49–67.

Deffenbacher, J. L. 1994. "Anger Reduction: Issues, Assessment, and Intervention Strategies." In *Anger, Hostility and the Heart,* edited by A. W. Siegman and T. W. Smith. Hillsdale, NJ: Lawrence Erlbaum.

Deffenbacher, J. L., E. R. Oetting, M. F. Huff, G. R. Cornell, and C. J Dillinger. 1996. "Evaluation of Two Cognitive Behavioral Approaches to General Anger Reduction." *Cognitive Therapy and Research* 20: 551–573.

Deffenbacher, J. L., and M. McKay. 2000. *Overcoming Situational and General Anger.* Oakland, CA: New Harbinger Publications.

Foa, E., E. Hembree, and B. Olaslov Rothbaum. 2007. *Prolonged Exposure Therapy for PTSD: Emotional Processing of Traumatic Experience, Therapist Guide.* Oxford: Oxford University Press.

Fraizer, J. C. 2017. "Comprehensive Coping Inventory: A Study of Concurrent Validity and Clinical Utility." Dissertation, The Wright Institute.

Frank, R. I., and J. Davidson. 2014. *The Transdiagnostic Road Map to Case Formulation and Treatment Planning: Practical Guidance for Clinical Decision Making.* Oakland, CA: New Harbinger Publications.

Freeman, A., J. Pretzer, B. Flemming, and K. Simon. 2004. *Clinical Applications of Cognitive Therapy.* New York: Plenum.

Gilbert, P. 2014. *Mindful Compassion.* Oakland, CA: New Harbinger Publications.

Greenberger, D., and C. Padesky. 1995. *Mind Over Mood.* New York: Guilford Press.

Gross, J. J. 1998. "The Emerging Field of Emotion Regulation: An Integrative Review." *Review of General Psychology* 2(3): 271–299.

Harvey, A. G., E. Watkins, and W. Mansell. 2004. *Cognitive Behavioral Processes Across Psychological Disorders: A Transdiagnostic Approach to Research and Treatment.* NY: Oxford University Press.

Hayes, S. C., K. Strosahl, and K. Wilson. 1999. *Acceptance and Commitment Therapy: An Experimental Approach to Behavior Change.* New York: Guilford Press.

Hayes, S. C., and S. Hofmann. 2018. *Process-Based CBT.* Oakland, CA: New Harbinger Publications.

Hayes, S. C., and S. Smith. 2005. *Get Out Of Your Mind and Into Your Life.* Oakland, CA: New Harbinger Publications.

Hopko, D. R., C. W. Lejuez, K. J. Ruggiero, and G. H. Eifert. 2003. "Contemporary Behavioral Activation Treatments for Depression: Procedures, Principles, and Progress." *Clinical Psychology Review* 23(5): 699–717.

Kabat-Zinn, J. 1995. *Mindfulness meditation.* New York: Nightingale-Conant Corporation.

Kabat-Zinn, J., A. O. Massion, J. Kristeller, L. G. Peterson, K. Fletcher, L. Pbert, W. Linderking, and S. F. Santorelli. 1992. "Effectiveness of Meditation-Based Stress Reduction Program in the Treatment of Anxiety Disorders." *American Journal of Psychiatry* 149(7): 936–943.

Kolts, R. L. 2016. *CFT Made Simple: A Clinician's Guide to Practicing Compassion-Focused Therapy.* Oakland, CA: New Harbinger Publications.

Linehan, M. 1993. *Cognitive Behavioral Therapy of Borderline Personality Disorder.* New York: Guilford Press.

Mahoney, M. 1974. *Cognition and Behavior Modification.* Cambridge, MA: Ballinger Publishing Company.

Martell, C. R., S. Dimidjian, and R. Herman-Dunn. 2013. *Behavioral Activation for Depression: A Clinician's Guide.* New York: Guilford Press.

McKay, M., and A. West. 2016. *Emotion Efficacy Therapy.* Oakland, CA: Context Press.

McKay, M., and J. Wood. 2019. *The New Happiness.* Oakland, CA: New Harbinger Publications.

McKay, M., J. Wood, and J. Brantley. 2019. *The Dialectical Behavior Therapy Skills Workbook,* 2nd ed. Oakland, CA: New Harbinger Publications.

McKay, M., M. Davis, and P. Fanning. 2021. *Thoughts & Feelings: Taking Control of Your Moods and Your Life,* 5th ed. Oakland, CA: New Harbinger Publications.

McKay, M., and P. D. Rogers. 2000. *The Anger Control Workbook.* Oakland, CA: New Harbinger Publications.

McKay, M., P. Zurita Ona, and P. Fanning. 2012. *Mind and Emotions: A Universal Treatment for Emotional Disorders.* Oakland, CA: New Harbinger Publications.

Meichenbaum, D. 1985. *Stress Inoculation Training.* New York: Pergamon Press.

Neff, K. 2011. *Self-Compassion: The Proven Power of Being Kind to Yourself.* New York: HarperCollins.

Neff, K., and C. Germer. 2018. *The Mindful Self-Compassion Workbook: A proven Way to Accept Yourself, Build Inner Strength, and Thrive.* New York: Guilford Press.

Nolen-Hoeksema, S., and E. R. Watkins. 2011. "A Heuristic for Developing Transdiagnostic Models of Psychopathology: Explaining Multifinality and Divergent Trajectories." *Perspectives on Psychological Science* 6(6): 589–609.

Persons, J. B., J. Davidson, M. A. Tompkins, and E. T. Dowd. 2001. *Essential Components of Cognitive-Behavior Therapy for Depression.* Washington, DC: American Psychological Association.

Pool, E. S. 2021. "The CCI-55: An Updated Assessment Tool for Transdiagnostic Treatment." Dissertation, The Wright Institute.

Salkovskis, P. M. 1996. "The Cognitive Approach to Anxiety: Threat Beliefs, Safety-Seeking Behavior, and the Special Case of Health anxiety and Obsessions." In *Frontiers of Cognitive Therapy,* edited by P. M. Salkovskis. New York: Guilford Press.

Seif, M. N. and S. Winston. 2014. *What Every Therapist Needs to Know about Anxiety Disorders: Key Concepts, Insights, and Interventions.* Oxfordshire, UK: Routledge.

Seligman, M. E. P., and M. Csikszentmihalyi. 2000. "Positive Psychology: An Introduction." *American Psychologist* 55(1): 5–14.

Shapiro, S. L., and G. E. Schwartz. 2000. "The Role of Intention in Self-Regulation: Toward Intentional Systemic Mindfulness." In *Handbook of Self-Regulation,* edited by M. Zeidner, P. R. Pintrich, and M. Boekaerts. San Diego, CA: Academic Press.

Shekelle, R. B., M. Gale, A. M. Ostfeld, and O. Paul. 1983. "Hostility, Risk of CHD, and Mortality." *Psychosomatic Medicine* 45: 109–114.

Sydenham, M., J. Beardwood, and K. Rimes. 2017. "Beliefs about Emotions, Depression, Anxiety and Fatigue: A Mediational Analysis." *Behavioural and Cognitive Psychotherapy* 45(1): 73–78. https://doi.org/10.1017/S1352465816000199

Titchener, E. B. 1916. *Textbook of Psychology.* New York: Macmillan.

Wells, A. 2009. *Metacognitive Therapy for Anxiety and Depression.* New York: Guilford Press.

Zettle, R. D. (2007). *ACT for Depression: A Clinician's Guide to Using Acceptance and Commitment Therapy in Treating Depression.* Oakland, CA: New Harbinger Publications

Zurita Ona, P. E. 2007. "Development and Validation of a Comprehensive Coping Inventory." Dissertation, The Wright Institute.

About the Author

Matthew McKay, PhD, is a professor at the Wright Institute in Berkeley, CA. He has authored and coauthored numerous books, including *The Dialectical Behavior Therapy Skills Workbook*, *Self-Esteem*, and *Couple Skills*, which have sold more than four million copies combined. He received his PhD in clinical psychology from the California School of Professional Psychology, and specializes in the cognitive behavioral treatment of anxiety and depression.

Patrick Fanning is a professional writer in the mental health field, and founder of a men's support group in Northern California. He has authored and coauthored twelve self-help books, including *Self-Esteem*, *Thoughts and Feelings*, *Couple Skills*, and *Mind and Emotions*.

Erica Pool, PsyD, earned her doctorate at the Wright Institute in Berkeley, CA; and has clinical and research experience at the University of California, Berkeley, and the VA Northern California Health Care System; and has consulted with mental health start-ups. The goal of her work is to understand processes at the core of human suffering to help craft individualized and culturally responsive treatments.

Patricia E. Zurita Ona, PsyD, "Dr. Z," is a psychologist specializing in working with and creating compassionate, research-based, and actionable resources for overachievers and overthinkers to get them unstuck from worries, fears, anxieties, perfectionism, procrastination, obsessions, and ineffective "playing it safe" actions. She is founder of the East Bay Behavior Therapy Center—a boutique practice where she offers therapy and coaching services based on acceptance and commitment therapy (ACT) and contextual behavioral science. She has been nominated as a fellow of the Association of Contextual Behavioral Science for her contributions to the applications of ACT to specific fear-based struggles.

ABOUT US

Founded by psychologist Matthew McKay and Patrick Fanning, New Harbinger has published books that promote wellness in mind, body, and spirit for more than forty-five years.

Our proven-effective self-help books and pioneering workbooks help readers of all ages and backgrounds make positive lifestyle changes, improve mental health and well-being, and achieve meaningful personal growth. In addition, our spirituality books offer profound guidance for deepening awareness and cultivating healing, self-discovery, and fulfillment.

New Harbinger is proud to be an independent and employee-owned company, publishing books that reflect its core values of integrity, innovation, commitment, sustainability, compassion, and trust. Written by leaders in the field and recommended by therapists worldwide, New Harbinger books are practical, reliable, and provide real tools for real change.

newharbingerpublications

MORE BOOKS from
NEW HARBINGER PUBLICATIONS

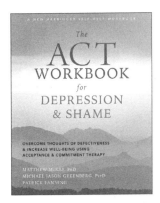

**THE ACT WORKBOOK FOR
DEPRESSION AND SHAME**

Overcome Thoughts of Defectiveness
and Increase Well-Being Using
Acceptance and Commitment Therapy

978-1684035540 / US $22.95

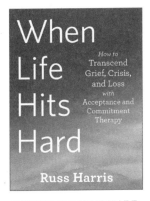

WHEN LIFE HITS HARD

How to Transcend Grief, Crisis,
and Loss with Acceptance and
Commitment Therapy

978-1684039012 / US $19.95

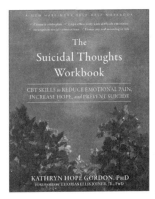

**THE SUICIDAL THOUGHTS
WORKBOOK**

CBT Skills to Reduce Emotional Pain,
Increase Hope, and Prevent Suicide

978-1684037025 / US $21.95

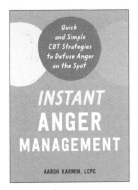

**INSTANT ANGER
MANAGEMENT**

Quick and Simple CBT Strategies
to Defuse Anger on the Spot

978-1684038398 / US $14.95

CAN'T STOP THINKING

How to Let Go of Anxiety and
Free Yourself from
Obsessive Rumination

978-1684036776 / US $18.95

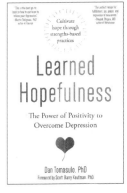

LEARNED HOPEFULNESS

The Power of Positivity to
Overcome Depression

978-1684034680 / US $16.95

 newharbingerpublications
1-800-748-6273 / newharbinger.com

(VISA, MC, AMEX / prices subject to change without notice)
Follow Us 🅾 🇫 🐦 ▶ 📌 in

Did you know there are **free tools** you can download for this book?

Free tools are things like **worksheets, guided meditation exercises**, and **more** that will help you get the most out of your book.

You can download free tools for this book—whether you bought or borrowed it, in any format, from any source—from the New Harbinger website. All you need is a NewHarbinger.com account. Just use the URL provided in this book to view the free tools that are available for it. Then, click on the "download" button for the free tool you want, and follow the prompts that appear to log in to your NewHarbinger.com account and download the material.

You can also save the free tools for this book to your **Free Tools Library** so you can access them again anytime, just by logging in to your account! Just look for this button on the book's free tools page.

+ Save this to my free tools library